Wheels, Skis and Floats

Wheels, Skis and Floats
The Northern Adventures of a Pioneer Pilot

by
E. C. (Ted) Burton
and
Robert S. Grant

*Based on an original manuscript by Edward Cherry Burton, Sr.,
including sketches and doggerrel by E. C. Burton, Sr.*

hancock
house

ISBN 0-88839-428-4

Cataloging in Publication Data
Burton, E. C. (Edward Cherry), 1931 -
Wheels, skis and floats
Includes bibliographical references and index.
ISBN 0-88839-428-4

1. Burton, E. C. (Edward Cherry), 1931 - 2. Air pilots—
Canada—Biography. I. Grant, Robert S. II. Title.
TL540.B78A3 1998   629.13'092   C98-910501-6

Printed in Canada—Jasper Printers

Editor: Nancy Miller
Production: Dallas Hyndman
Cover Painting: Cher Hogan

*We acknowledge the financial support of the Government of Canada through the
Book Publishing Industry Development Program for our publishing activities.*

Published simultaneously in Canada and the United States by

HANCOCK HOUSE PUBLISHERS LTD.
19313 Zero Avenue, Surrey, B.C. V4P 1M7
(604) 538-1114 Fax (604) 538-2262
HANCOCK HOUSE PUBLISHERS
1431 Harrison Avenue, Blaine, WA 98230
(604) 538-1114 Fax (604) 538-2262
Web Site: www.hancockhouse.com *email:* sales@hancockhouse.com

Contents

Dedication

Ed Burton Sr. would certainly have intended to dedicate his memoirs to his wife Lucille, who cheerfully put up with the hardships, innumerable moves and dangers and uncertainties of his chosen career. For many years their only possessions were the bare necessities that could be crammed into the cabin of a small airplane. Without her support, he would not have been able to indulge his passion for a life in aviation.

The authors recognize that any success they have achieved in their endeavors and in the production of this book are largely due to the help, support and encouragement of their wives.

This book, then, is dedicated with gratitude to Linda Grant and Erica Burton, and to the memory of Ed and Lucille who made it all happen.

Introduction

This book has its origins in a 20,000-word manuscript written in the late 1940s by Edward Cherry Burton. Revised and expanded from time to time, it was never published. After Burton's death in 1966, his wife, Lucille, a newspaper journalist, and son, Ted, a Northern Ontario Crown attorney, attempted publication without success.

In late 1994, Ted and Erica Burton contacted Robert (Bob) S. Grant and his wife, Linda. Knowing that Bob, a Canadair CL-215 water bomber pilot, was a widely published aviation writer with serious interests in civil aviation history, the Burtons showed the manuscript to the Grants. Bob's interest was immediate. The Burtons, including Lucille, made an agreement with the Grants to rewrite the manuscript as a joint effort. Bob would be the acknowledged creative director.

Bob decided, and the Burtons agreed, that the manuscript suited a biography on the career of Edward Cherry Burton. The next decision involved the material. Aside from the original manuscript, the Burtons supplied newspaper clippings, photographs and Lucille's and Ted's recollections of events as originally described by Edward Burton, who had been a great raconteur.

As a writer, Bob already had an extensive collection of materials concerning early aircraft. He expanded this knowledge by researching Ottawa's National Archives, Public Archives of Manitoba, Hudson's Bay Company Archives and the Western Canada Aviation Museum's catalogue in Winnipeg.

The story of Ed's early adventures as a homesteader in the Onion Lake District of Saskatchewan, including a shooting episode, came from descendants of Ed's friends and neighbors of 1912. A bonanza of first-hand information about mail flying and the Mitchell Expedition was discovered in a cache of letters, complete with poems and sketches, written to Lucille. Ed's meticulous pilot logbooks provided dates, locations and names.

The biography of Edward Cherry Burton, then, is as accurate as possible considering the original manuscript was first drafted over half a century ago.

The actual writing of *Wheels, Skis and Floats* became a cooperative affair. Bob took original chapters and rewrote them with additional material gleaned from his research. Ted, with an eye for detail, corrected and supplemented where necessary, then bounced his results back to Bob for final consideration.

Every chapter underwent several such collaborations. Occasionally, Ted varied the process by doing a first rewrite. Linda took responsibility for most of the word processing and at each stage, Linda and Erica contributed input on style, suitable content, and of course, every writer's bugaboo, spelling. When nearing the final draft, they called upon retired superintendent of education William Colborne in Thunder Bay for comments. His suggestions added grace and cohesion to the final product. For his efforts, the Burtons and Grants are extremely grateful.

The authors believe the book is important at the close of the twentieth century when much of mankind has been challenged by radically changing lifestyles. This is not so much because *Wheels, Skis and Floats* is a history, but because it relates how one individual with grit not only survived but succeeded in living a satisfying life while dealing with the dangers and uncertainties of his occupation in a tumultuous era.

Edward Cherry Burton made a career of flying small, prone-to-fail airplanes in lonesome places for thirty-nine years, dying with his boots off. Many of his contemporaries either left the profession early or died in flaming wrecks. The safe haven of a bland city life or the profitable, but disreputable, aerial rum-running or alien smuggling was not his style. Edward Cherry Burton lived a good life and lived it well.

This is his story.

CHAPTER ONE

Farming Life to Flying Lessons

In the early summer of 1912, rich pasture land cradled the village of Harlan, Saskatchewan, fourteen miles north of the North Saskatchewan River. Wolf-willow and wild roses scented the air and clumps of young poplar dotted the nearby grassy uplands. To the east, the rounded slope of Frenchman's Butte dominated the skyline.

Twenty-one-year-old homesteader Edward Cherry Burton stood forlorn among crops trampled and fences smashed by cattle driven over them by a belligerent neighbor. Since Burton's arrival in Canada in 1909, the neighbor and his sons had tried to force the young Englishman from his land. A few days earlier, they had dragged him behind a horse. Badly scraped and battered, he managed to free himself and crawl into the brush. They left him there, threatening to return and repeat the deed.

In the stillness of a morning not yet tainted by prairie dust and stifling heat, three men on horseback thundered over a ridge. The anguished young Burton recognized the neighbor and sons, and quickly drew a revolver from a holster strapped to his plough. The older man, seeing the gun, uncoiled a long, grease-slicked rope and kicked his horse forward. Defying Burton to shoot, he laughed and the three intruders lunged forward.

With scrapes on his face and forearms still unhealed, Burton knew he would never survive another dragging. With no other choice, he fired and saw the older man fall dead to the ground. The two sons fled. Distraught, Burton rode twelve miles to the Onion Lake Mission near the Sekaskooch and Makaoo Reserves.

Dr. Elizabeth Matheson, one of Canada's first woman doctors and an acting coroner, had patched Burton up after the first incident and now advised him to report to the storied and widely respected Canadian "mounties" or Royal North-West Mounted Police (RNWMP). He found them waiting, confident they would not be called upon to track him down.

The situation hardly seemed a fitting one for a young English gentleman. Edward Burton was held on his own recognizance in stables adjacent to the RNWMP barracks at Lloydminster. Burton's close friend, homesteader Earl Goodman, whom he had known during his school days in England, circulated a petition for leniency. The deceased had been an unpopular American bully who harassed settlers along the grassy uplands of the North Saskatchewan River valley. Instead of working the land, he chose to drive out whomever he could and acquire their properties at below-value prices.

The court acquitted Burton for reasons of self-defence. When the clerk read the verdict, fellow settlers stood and applauded. Burton returned to stuking wheat, chasing cattle and digging post holes, but soon realized he could never settle back into the routine of Saskatchewan farm life. The RNWMP warned him that the dead man had friends who might not look kindly on Burton's homesteading efforts. They suggested politely that he move on.

Burton's decision to leave Harlan eventually led him to an exciting and fulfilling career in the Canadian skies. With the same adventurous spirit that brought him from English country lanes to Saskatchewan sod, he excelled as one of Canada's earliest aviation pioneers. At great risk, Burton carried airmail through black nights, airlifted northerners from tiny lakes, skirted flickering thunderstorms and ventured into regions and conditions few airmen had ever penetrated.

Edward was born in Redhill, England, to George Burton and Grace Mary Padwick on April 15, 1891, one of five children. His sea captain father had traveled the world on sailing ships and later, as a master of a Cunard White Star steamship. One of George Burton's older sons became a Pentecostal minister in the Belgian Congo, another moved to Canada as a gentleman farmer. A daughter became a nurse in Ceylon and another daughter remained in England.

Edward, as the youngest son, was also encouraged to seek his fortune abroad. He arrived on the prairies on his eighteenth birthday to spend an unhappy year as a worker indentured to an autocratic farmer. The beginning proved almost unbearable but "Ed" learned the rudiments of farming and did as he was told. When his time expired, he claimed a piece of land for himself. During months of back-breaking toil, the hardened young Brit managed to cultivate a few lonely acres before the American tough destroyed his property.

On leaving the Canadian west after the horrifying encounter with violence and death, he used his English education and farming experience to sell Delco electric plants in rural regions near Toronto and London. In August, 1914, however, Burton's life changed again when England and her allies went to war against the German-led Central Powers and young men across the Dominion of Canada responded to the call of duty. Now 23, Burton decided to enlist as an infantryman.

To his dismay, army doctors diagnosed him as having "hammer toes," a painful deformity in which the toes became highly arched and misaligned. This, declared the recruiting officer, prevented him from becoming an efficient infantryman. He would be unable to march and, as everyone knew, all good soldiers marched.

Undeterred by rejection, Burton considered the Royal Flying Corps (RFC) and discovered that a candidate needed a pilot's license before joining. Keen to take up his part in the war effort and drawn to flying, he determined to do both. Unable to afford civilian training, Burton returned to making a living as a bookkeeper for several corporations in Toronto. As Burton's son later said, his father spent "...a couple of years in limbo" and strongly felt his exclusion from the war.

While Ed Burton pushed pencils, the RFC in Great Britain was learning the hard lessons of aerial warfare. In the beginning, British airmen held their own against the dreaded hun. But as Germany developed faster and better-armed airplanes, Allied casualty rates soared. Replacement air crew for the fabric-covered flying machines became scarce and recruiters began snatching men wherever they could. By mid-1916, the pilot license prerequisite had been dropped and the RFC began advertising for the "All Seeing Aviator."

Canada appeared to be the answer to Great Britain's shortage of manpower. During a conference at Adastra House, England, on December 21, 1916, top military officials created the "Royal

Flying Corps, Canada." A month later, the first contingent of British officers and staff arrived in Saint John, New Brunswick. Under the command of 34-year-old Lt. Col. Cuthbert Gurney Hoare, they left the sooty port and boarded a Toronto-bound train to organize Canadian flight training. Royal Flying Corps posters plastered throughout the Canadian countryside encouraged Burton to try again.

Young men, he learned, were expected to be clear-headed and between eighteen and thirty years of age with grounding in algebra and geometry. The officer corps demanded that each candidate be "able to speak the King's English," as well as "bear the ear marks of a gentleman." One forthright recruiter put it more succinctly when he snapped "clean bred young charges with lots of the devil!"

Burton, educated at Trent College before leaving England, qualified in spite of his hammer toes. As "Flying Cadet 74635," he would earn $1.10 per day and up to fifty cents per hour flying pay. He soon discovered that becoming an RFC cadet entailed far more than manipulating the joysticks of dashing airplanes depicted on the recruiting posters.

Assigned to a 350-acre training camp called Mohawk Field near the community of Deseronto, 130 miles east of Toronto, Burton counted three squadrons or fifty-four airplanes based there. Twelve flight sheds housed the aircraft and served as shelters for ground school instruction. Nearly 300 cadets per month flew their first solos from Mohawk and the nearby sister airstrip, Camp Rathbun.

Burton began the accelerated process of becoming a fighter pilot with 43 Wing 85 Canadian Training Squadron or CTS on October 13, 1917. Dressed in the distinctive RFC double-breasted tunic, cheese-cutter cap and high, spit-polished leather boots, which were a concession to the defunct cavalry, he spent hours on drill parades. The object, several sergeant-majors bawled, was "to make soldiers out of you as quickly as possible." The RFC had evidently forgotten about hammer toes.

"The first instruction in ground school consisted of classes and lectures in theory of flight, map reading, bomb dropping and aerial photography," Burton recalled. "We were taught the use of wireless telegraph and to practice its use until attaining efficiency in sending and receiving messages."

The future officers attended lectures on such nonflying topics as mess etiquette and sail making. Instructors soon began directing cadets in the handling of lethal tools like Lewis and Vickers machine guns. They learned, too, the basics of airplane engines, undercarriages and instruments before strapping into a special ground-based trainer with joystick, rudder pedals and pilot seat. At the end of the program, quartermasters issued leather helmets and glass goggles. With fifteen others, Burton advanced to flight training at Camp Rathbun.

Almost all RFC training in Canada took place in two-seat, 90-hp airplanes designed by American Glen Curtiss. Called "Jennies," a phonetic corruption of the Curtiss JN series, the type's first flight took place in 1914. Before long, the cotton-covered, wire-braced Jenny caught the attention of the RFC. On December 15, 1916, Toronto's Canadian Aeroplanes Ltd. acquired its manufacturing rights and produced the JN-4 (Cdn) model, which was referred to as the "Canuck." Nine manufacturers in the United States and Canada produced over 4,100 Jennies.

The Canadian-built Jenny prototype went into service on February 22, 1917. State-of-the-art, its upper wing span measured 43-feet, 7 3/8-inches and the length, 27-feet, 2 1/2-inches. Empty, it weighed 1,390 pounds, and on takeoff it could gross 1,920 pounds and climb to 2,500 feet in ten minutes. The instructor rode in the rear cockpit and the student settled into the front. Burton's first instructional flight took only ten minutes in Curtiss JN-4 No. 420.

"As we had no means of communications, instruction had to be by signals," said Burton. "The instructor kicked the back of the seat in front of him to gain attention and indicated with a jerk of his thumb that one wing was too high or too low."

After eight lessons totalling only two and a half hours, Lt. McCallum sent Burton aloft on his own in Curtiss JN-4 No. 334 on October 17, 1917. His first solo was uneventful but Burton kept a wary eye on the confidence-inspiring "Hungry Lizzie," a twelve-cylinder Packard ambulance festooned with axes, saws and wire cutters, stationed at the corner of the airfield.

"Although our instructors told us the Curtiss Jenny was supposed to be an easy airplane to fly, some of the cadets seemed to go out of their way to hurt themselves," said Burton. "One brash, overconfident young one bragged that a pilot's first solo wasn't really anything special. On his first time alone up there, he said he'd perform a loop."

The cadets watched the Jenny take off across the grass aerodrome and climb to 1,500 feet. From level flight, the nose went down to gather speed and then the self-professed expert abruptly brought the control stick back to enter the loop, but his rough handling caused the airplane to flip on its back. As the horrified students looked on, the frantic cadet could not recover and whirled down inverted.

"The plane was still spinning when it ploughed into the ground," said Burton. "Hungry Lizzie was soon there to pick up what remained of the cadet and the wrecking truck picked up what was left of the Jenny."

Accidents were not unusual for enthusiastic recruits expecting to become glamorous knights of the skies. Intense training in double-quick time caused numerous mishaps. During a twenty-one-day stretch, nineteen cadets and instructors died as Jennies smashed into stump-filled fields, tangled with fog-covered trees or collided with assorted objects like cow barns and slow-moving locomotives.

Burton witnessed one pupil destroy his undercarriage after neglecting to level off while landing. After cussing him out, the cadet's instructor sent him aloft again. This time, the harried youngster hit the ground hard enough to smash the wheels into the lower wings. Following more cursing from the instructor but still with no refresher training, he took off once more in a third Jenny and landed safely. The student, William Davis, became Burton's employer and lifelong friend two decades later in Quebec.

During Burton's early training, students were given no instruction in spin recovery. The lucky few who saved themselves could not explain what movements they used during their frantic gyrations in twisting, earth-bound Jennies. Lecturers discussed the maneuver in ground school but as S. F. Wise said in his *Canadian Airmen and the First World War*, Vol. 1, pupils were told simply to remove their hands and feet from the controls. The airplane would supposedly recover by itself.

The "let-it-go" method worked in some of the more stable airplanes of later years, but spins cost the RFC many lives before someone discovered the correct procedure. All pilots had to do was move the stick forward, apply opposite rudder to the direction of the spin then ease gently out of the dive.

"One instructor, afraid we cadets would consider the Jennies as unstable death traps, came up with his own pretty flamboyant confidence-instilling measure," Burton said. "In flight, he'd climb out of his cockpit and sit on the lower wing. Whether or not his crazy teaching technique saved lives may have been hard to say, but it left no doubt for us as to who was the pilot-in-command."

After elementary flying camp, cadets learned advanced map reading and put into practice the tedious lectures from ground school. Written examinations for advanced studies required 80 percent pass marks and the recording of eight words per minute in morse code.

In the air, Burton moved on to the deadly art of dog fighting. Part of the course included clearing stoppages from cantankerous machine guns while thousands of feet above the ground. He also learned to cooperate with ground-based artillery units to range targets with coded signals. His aerial gunnery lessons consisted of shooting at targets towed behind a Jenny. The RFC discontinued the practice when too many towplanes landed with holed fuselages and shredded rudders.

While Burton mastered the Ontario skies as a budding fighter pilot, negotiations were underway for Canada's cadets to escape the uncomfortable open cockpits of winter flying. Royal Flying Corps staff drew up a reciprocal agreement with the U.S. Army to train ten American squadrons. Canadians would be assigned to various flying fields in the warmer southern climate. At first, it appeared the RFC would move training wings to Florida but instead, opted for locations near Fort Worth, Texas.

On September 24, 1917, the first RFC officers left Toronto by train, arriving at Fort Worth several days later with twenty-four crated Jennies. More staff followed when Deseronto's 43 Wing pulled into Fort Worth on November 17. When they arrived, construction of sub aerodromes had barely begun. Unfinished barracks and lack of proper water supplies forced the hardy Canadian cadets to spend the initial weeks in tents. Those with rural backgrounds had little trouble roughing it, but the city boys suffered in the cold and mud.

Burton's first flight over the Texas cattle ranges took place from Everman aerodrome in Curtiss Jenny No. C785. As part of his navigation training, he logged 106 landings at nearby airstrips in sixty-seven hours flying time by the end of 1917.

"After all of us in 43 Wing finished our training, most of the pilots and mechanics got overseas postings. I didn't, and I went through every hoop and trick I could think of to get sent over," said Burton.

Headquarters overruled his persistent requests for overseas work and ordered him to an instructor's posting. This was an exceptional decision for the time; most flying instructors had European wartime experience before teaching novices to fly. In Burton's case, his extraordinary abilities were evident when a *Mail & Empire* reporter characterized him as "the gamest and the best of the embryo pilots."

Forced to remain at Camp Everman, Ed was disappointed that he would never fly above the fields of Belgium and France. Nevertheless, he became part of an elite group handpicked for one of the most important tasks in military history.

"They are the big leaguers of those going through training; everyday they give the best that in them is, and teach the uniniti-ated all there is—looping, rolling, spinning and a clear eye and steady hand," added the *Mail & Empire* reporter.

At this stage of the war, techniques and equipment showed vast improvement through the experience gained in Canadian flight schools. Spinning was no longer considered fatal. The training syllabus now included routine spin entries and recover-ies before first solo. To help get their points across above the roar of the Jenny's eight-cylinder OX-5 engine, instructors communi-cated through a wondrous speaking tube made from surgical rub-ber hose connected to ear covers in the student's helmet.

Pilots learned to fly by "feel." Encouraged to listen to the sound of the wind in the wires, they sensed the subtle vibrations when adjusting throttles or moving the nose up or down to correct airspeed. Instrument panels held little more than a revolution counter, oil pressure gauge and altimeter, and students were told to stay clear of cloud. Some soloed with as much as six hours dual and others went aloft with as little as forty-five minutes.

The RFC encouraged a high degree of independence and decision-making from pilots. Occasionally, a few lacked resourcefulness. Instructors and cadets noted a spectacular example when they looked up at a Jenny flying across the aerodrome with full throttle. Barely missing a hangar, the pilot pulled up and came around again.

"When he repeated the performance several times, we could see he was in difficulty and not just fooling around," Burton explained. "He was wearing a cadet's crash helmet and had his face over the side as he dashed by, frantically yelling something which, of course, we couldn't hear."

Burton and his fellow instructors realized the Jenny's throttle had become disconnected from the engine and the cadet was unable to throttle back. Burton ordered a gang of students to rush to a nearby hangar and bring out the wing of a dismantled Jenny. Someone else ran for a brush and a pot of paint.

Across the wing, they hastily dabbed "Switch Off" and held it up for the panicked pilot. He read the gigantic letters and immediately shut off his engine. Above the middle of the field, he lacked enough maneuvering room to turn around and complete a safe gliding approach. After a reasonably smooth landing at high speed, the JN-4 slammed into the side of a building.

"Another trip for Hungry Lizzie," remarked Burton.

Instructors never allowed the pall of death to hang over the camp for long. Whenever fatalities occurred or spectacular crashes took place, every cadet nearby was mustered immediately into an airplane and sent away to fly.

When the Texas training program ended, Burton returned to Canada on April 19, 1918. Posted to Leaside, north of Toronto, he flew dozens of short instructional flights. Other brief trips included test hops after maintenance inspections. When downed

Jennies had been hastily repaired in a distant field after forced landings, Burton was selected to fly them back to Leaside. In fact, his leather-covered logbook showed numerous entries when his own engine stopped and compelled him to land in pastures far from base.

His friend Jack Leach provided a colorful break in the routine of flying training. A quaint character who had lost a leg years before in an industrial accident, he flew fighters in France before assignment as an instructor. During an aerobatics display in a Jenny, Leach misjudged his distance from the ground, scraped the wing tip and cartwheeled. As the airplane settled into an untidy pile of splinters, a Hungry Lizzie raced across the field. When the attendant jumped out, Leach was extricating himself from the crumpled cockpit.

"Are you hurt, Sir? Are you hurt?" the excited attendant yelled.

"I've broken my bloody leg," snapped Leach.

"Bring the stretcher, Bill, he broke his leg!" the attendant screamed at the Lizzie's driver.

"Never mind the god-damn stretcher," shouted Leach. "Bring me a hammer and nails so I can fix it myself!"

Leach told Burton he had destroyed five peg legs in airplane crashes. In 1930, he broke it for the last time while attempting some prohibited low-level aerobatics at Port Arthur (now Thunder Bay) on Lake Superior. After a night-long party at a pilots' mecca called the Prince Arthur Hotel, he flew two successful loops but did not leave enough height for recovery on the third. Two passengers died with Leach when the Hamilton H-47 seaplane slammed almost vertically into the water.

While serving at Leaside with 43 Wing's 78 Canadian Training Squadron, Burton became involved in a series of airmail flights. Captain Brian A. Peck and Corporal C. W. Matthews had already completed Canada's first airmail delivery when they flew from Montreal to Leaside on June 20, 1918, with 124 letters and a case of "Old Mull" whisky for a Toronto wedding which "cried out to be toasted in distilled spirits."

The trip, organized by the Montreal branch of the Aerial League of the British Empire, helped draw in new recruits for the

Royal Air Force, as the Royal Flying Corps became known on April 1, 1918, and also demonstrated a new public service.

The Aero Club of Canada decided to focus on the feasibility of inter-city mail service with three Jenny flights. According to historian R. K. Malott, it was fitting that Canada's capital serve as a landing site. The honor of the first run to Ottawa went to 78 CTS's Lt. Tremper Longman on August 15, 1918. After a trouble-free flight, he returned to Leaside two days later, eliminating the need for a ten-hour train trip.

The next successful delivery took place on August 26 by Lt. Arthur M. Dunstan. After a fuel stop in Deseronto, he landed at Ottawa and returned to Leaside the next day. Like most Jennies, Lt. Dunstan's Canadian-built No. 282 with "Winnipeg" painted in bold red letters on both sides, cruised at 2,000 feet and carried a useful load of 484 pounds including pilot.

On September 4 at 8:00 A.M., Burton began the third and last trial flight from Leaside in *Winnipeg* with 44 letters. Like Longman and Dunstan, he stopped at Deseronto to top off his fuel tank and replenish the Jenny's radiator before continuing to Rockcliffe Rifle Range in Ottawa. There, he refueled again from a load of milk cans delivered by the Imperial Oil Company on a horse-drawn wagon. A photograph of the crowd at Rockcliffe showed the unmistakable figure of young MacKenzie King, later to become Canada's prime minister, standing beside the Jenny.

After a brief lunch, Burton coaxed the Jenny back into the air carrying a small bag of envelopes which were replies to the letters he had flown to Ottawa. Following a compass course to Brockville, he picked up the St. Lawrence River, flew to Lake Ontario and parallelled the shore.

"The engine was throttled back to 1,375 revolutions and gave no trouble," Burton commented in his official report. "The airspeed indicator registered a speed of fifty-five miles per hour. Some time was lost on the outward journey owing to a slight headwind."

That evening, *Winnipeg* chugged toward Toronto, turned right south of the city and landed in Leaside at 6:40 P.M. Burton had completed Canada's first round trip air-mail flight in eight hours and five minutes flying time. The experiment demonstrated that a businessman could write to a customer and expect a reply the same day.

After the excitement of pioneering air-mail routes, Burton returned to his regular military duties. Flight instruction and testing rerigged, overhauled Jennies made up most of the work. Some days he flew seven different airplanes without incident until an early morning engine failure after takeoff in Curtiss JN-4 C197 resulted in a buckled undercarriage but with no human injuries.

Burton's last flight for the Royal Air Force (Canada) occurred in Curtiss JN-4 No. 1347 on November 23, 1918, at Long Branch aerodrome, eleven miles southwest of Toronto. When hostilities ceased on November 11, hundreds of men found themselves released from service. By the time Burton left No. 78 CTS, he had logged 617 landings in 241 hours in ninety-five Jennies. Burton was one of over 1,200 pilots trained in Canada.

With less than nineteen months of military service, Burton opted to remain in the downsizing RAF as long as possible. He traveled to England, allegedly to visit relatives but mainly to explore the possibilities of a permanent air force career. At No. 41 Training Depot Station, he flew Avro 504 3356, and two months later, took Avro 6763 from London to Northolt via Hendon. However, the RAF could not find a place for him, despite his experience. Only personnel with more seniority were retained.

On May 11, 1919, at the Crystal Palace headquarters of the Royal Air Force, Edward C. Burton was issued Army form Z.3 or a Protection Certificate releasing him from the armed forces. He listed his civilian occupation as rancher/salesman and requested repatriation to Canada.

After a lengthy rest, he surrendered his blue military embarkation card No. 5763 at Southampton on December 3, 1919, and boarded the ship *Caronia* for Canada.

CHAPTER TWO

Into the North with Big Bird

Edward Burton, often called "Ned" at this time in his life, returned to a peacetime country in which the public had not yet fully accepted air transportation. Automobile builders, railroad barons and shipping experts considered postwar aviation as the realm of clowns and daredevils. Indeed, war surplus relics and scruffy pilots seemed to prove their point as desperate men struggled to survive by selling rides advertised on gushing "Be a Bird" posters at fairs and exhibitions. Occasionally, however, incidents occurred which hinted at the future possibilities of a new industry.

On June 14, 1919, Capt. John Alcock and Lt. A. W. Brown left Newfoundland in a converted Vickers Vimy bomber for England. They made it. The fact that someone had flown across the Atlantic motivated Canadians to seriously consider the use of airplanes over bush country. A year later, Hector Dougall and Frank Ellis embarked from Winnipeg to The Pas with a paying passenger in an Avro 504—the first commercial flight into the northland.

Burton could not find a place to utilize his newly acquired skills and passion for flying. With no other choice, he returned to selling electric plants, this time from Listowel and Tillsonburg, Ontario.

In November, 1920, he took an accountant's position in Toronto which lasted seven months until the lure of the north overwhelmed him. If he could not fly, he resolved at least to escape dusty city streets, crowded sidewalks and time clocks.

Before homesteading in Harlan, Burton had traveled by rail through northern Ontario and had never forgotten its vast coniferous forests and innumerable tree-lined lakes. By chance, he heard of a timber-cutting company in need of a bookkeeper and before long, stepped from a CPR coach at Chapleau, 127 miles northwest of Sudbury, where he joined the Austin & Nicholson Lumber Company. Assigned to a manure-chinked, log-sided office deep in boreal bush south of the town, he copied tallies, recorded overtime and issued payroll cheques. In his leisure hours, he accompanied the bush-wise French-Canadian lumberjacks on log drives along the rushing rivers.

When not ice fishing or snowshoe tramping, Burton kept in touch with the outside world through ten-day-old newspapers that drifted into camp. Hunched beside blackened stove pipes and flickering coal oil lamps, he absorbed what he could of a slowly growing aviation industry.

Stories of early attempts to fly the Atlantic, the founding of Elliot Brothers Air Service at Hamilton and the Bishop-Barker Aerial Survey Company in Muskoka kept Burton's interest alive. During his self-imposed exile in the lumber camps, barnstorming and wing walking feats were also widely reported in the press.

By the time the tattered news sheets went to the outhouse for their final disposition, Burton knew what was happening across Canada. While daring pilots carried prospectors, trappers, priests or anyone interested in avoiding dog team and canoe travel, Burton waited for another chance at the controls of an airplane.

"Sometimes, I could hear airplane engines out there and found out that Laurentide Air Service Ltd. in Lac La Tortue, Quebec, had contracted with the Province of Ontario to provide detailed maps," Burton said. "The next year, they began moving fire fighters around and flying smoke patrols up as far as James Bay."

Laurentide's success encouraged the creation of the Ontario Provincial Air Service (OPAS) in May, 1924. Word through the forest "grapevine" reached the Austin & Nicholson Lumber Company that the newly formed organization needed aircrew. Burton bid his log-walled office good-bye and traveled to Sudbury where OPAS director Roy Maxwell accepted him as one of an elite group of pilots.

On May 17, 1924, under the guidance of check pilots Duke "Foghorn" Schiller, known for his ability to curse in bass clef, and Leigh Brintnell, later a president of MacKenzie Air Service Ltd. in Edmonton, he began learning the basics of flying boat handling. The training included tricky glassy water landings, a situation that left a pilot no visual reference from which to break a glide. If misjudged, a seaplane's nose could dig in and flip the craft over, trapping the occupants. At the other end of the scale, improper techniques in high winds and waves sometimes resulted in swamping and sinking.

Burton's first revenue trip with his new Commercial Air Pilot Certificate No. 198 took place on June 12, 1924, in Curtiss HS-2L G-CAOB from Port Arthur to Orient Bay, north of the community of Nipigon. The Curtiss, a flying boat originally used for submarine patrol during World War I, was designed by Glen Curtiss of Jenny fame. The "H-boats," as crews called the initial thirteen acquired by the OPAS, were first flown in October, 1917, as HS-1 models. The OPAS versions had seventy-four-foot, one-inch wing spans and were thirty-nine feet long.

Dubbed "flying squirrel cages" by mechanics because of the network of bracing wires in the wings, the average empty Curtiss HS-2L weighed 4,300 pounds. However, they became heavier each day as moisture seeped into their cedar-planked hulls. By the end of the season, they could barely be forced to leave the water. Mechanics pulled them out on a dolly to dry whenever possible.

As Burton began understanding the H-boat's eccentricities, he found the unwieldy machine carried 2,211.5 pounds on fire patrols, powered by a temperamental 400-hp, 12-cylinder Liberty engine. Water often spurted from the radiator and scalded the crew. Luckily, a plentiful supply of cooling water could always be found on the leaking cockpit floor and pumped back to the engine in flight.

The Liberty's rear-mounted, four-blade wood propeller produced a tremendous blast of air which yawed or turned the airplane to the right. As a remedy, most H-boats came equipped with a rubber cord attached to a fitting near the instrument panel. This lessened the effort necessary to compensate for the swing and made it easier for the pilot to maintain a straight takeoff path.

The mufflerless engine nearly deafened the crew who flew from the cockpit almost underneath it. The upper wing's bottom surface acted as a huge sounding board to reflect the roar directly onto the passengers. For hearing protection, all occupants wore thick ear cushions. Cramped beside each other the pilot and mechanic perspired heavily while on the surface and froze while aloft in spite of thick and bulky "Sidcot" suits. The front seat passenger had no protective windscreen and suffered from wind burn, cold and constant exposure to dampness.

Forced landings were routine, thanks to the Liberty's notorious unreliability. Without magnetos, the huge powerplant depended on a distributor and battery for spark. Consequently, failed generators or batteries meant instant loss of power. A generator change usually took two hours and replacing engines on remote lakes became routine.

"The mechanics were able to come up with a method of doing engine changes while the aircraft was floating on the water by sliding the engine down a diagonal brace to deck level, then sliding it on a ramp to a raft," said Burton, who greatly admired the "black gang" which kept the antiquated machines in the air. He enjoyed helping them whenever he could, and, in time, acquired his own mechanic's licence.

For navigation, H-boat pilots depended on huge ship-style compasses. Schiller soon pointed out that these clumsy devices lacked enough liquid to dampen the needle's oscillations. The fluid, he said, had evaporated. To compensate, he suggested filling them with alcohol. At the time, spirits could only be obtained with a medical prescription. Schiller, with his reputation as a connoisseur of fine liquors and his H-boat experience, managed to convince director Maxwell that only he could do the job. Armed with alcohol requisitions signed by authorities, Schiller and mechanic Al Cheesman became a popular pair, keeping the flying fraternity supplied with party refreshment.

Burton enjoyed the light-hearted, free-spirited camaraderie of some of Canada's most colorful aerial adventurers. In spite of Maxwell's prohibitions against alcoholic beverages and his insistence on proper deportment for his highly individualistic young men, they partied whenever they could. When their keen minds turned back to the serious business of manipulating awkward flying boats through northern Ontario skies, there were none better. The OPAS air crews, including Burton, became what one writer called a "highly effective nest" on which to pattern the future of Canadian aviation.

In the spring, the OPAS assigned pilots and mechanics to bases far from Sault Ste Marie headquarters. Burton flew fire patrols into virgin forest territories along the north shore of Lake

Superior from which pulp and paper mills received their raw materials. On June 22, after a brief flight test in G-CAOD, he was reassigned to Sioux Lookout. As the days warmed and winds dropped, he found that any lake he chose to land on had to be a long one. One pilot insisted the H-boat needed "a small ocean to become airborne." Also, pilots preferred sandy beaches; rocky shores easily punctured the wooden hulls.

Depositing fire crews did not come easily since the H-boat's lack of water rudders made steering difficult. To reach shore, the pilot steadied the nose in the general direction and hoped the hull would cut a straight line through the water. To turn, he pointed his arm to indicate where he wished to go. The mechanic then left his seat and made his way along the lower wing by groping from strut to strut and wire to wire. The weight forced the wing float into the water and the resultant drag caused a turn.

Hull damage became common, especially in the tea-colored lakes which characterized the countryside surrounding Sioux Lookout. Submerged rocks, drifting logs and hidden stumps damaged bottoms and wing tip sponsons, necessitating on-the-spot repairs. In one case, an H-boat swerved to avoid a motorboat and ran into a log boom. Holes and cracks were repaired with Le Page's Glue, candlewick packing and a magical compound called Stop-A-Leak. Brass nails finished the patch.

Although fire suppression and control justified a provincially owned air service for inhouse air transportation, numerous government branches began contacting Sioux Lookout base for access to the H-boats. Several calls came in to transport Department of Indian Affairs officials during treaty time. In the past, parties had traveled by canoe brigades, but now an airplane could cover in two hours what formerly took several days of paddling and portaging.

Few northerners, however, had been exposed to airplanes, especially ones as awesome and formidable as Curtiss HS-2Ls. When the huge yellow-winged birds chugged into sight with smoke blasting and barking from the Liberty's exhaust stacks, terrified Natives scattered into the bush. Even when shut down and tied to shore, black dripping blood (oil) and the pungent smell of gasoline inspired dread until curiosity finally overcame fear.

"One elder told me, 'Big bird, not much meat,' and another said that, 'The lazy white man always want to sit down to walk,'" laughed Burton, who felt warmly toward Canada's northern Natives. He treated them with dignity at a time when not every traveler could be counted on to do so.

After a few trips, the arrival of government airplanes became festive occasions. Crowds of Cree and Ojibway flocked to touch the wood and fabric "flying canoe." Sometimes, they did what one pilot called a "possum jig" to the accompaniment of leather drums and fiddles. The only solemnity occurred during the money presentation on Treaty Day when each man, woman and child received four dollars as agreed upon during historic signings between Her Majesty's representatives and the Indian peoples.

The airplane changed the lives of everyone in the north, Burton recalled. Aerial freighters hauled in trade goods and medevac flights became common as hundreds who had been shot, trapped or burned were taken to hospital within hours. One Sioux Lookout pilot returned to base ahead of schedule with an injured passenger who he believed needed immediate treatment.

"We secured the airplane to the dock, heaved the man out of the cockpit and set him down on a stretcher," Burton said. "He was a big man with one leg wrapped in a large bandage of sacking. He groaned and rolled his eyes, rocking back and forth as if he was really hurting."

An OPAS mechanic dashed to telephone the local hospital; someone ran to the cookhouse and brought the injured man a cup of coffee; another hurriedly readied the *Green Hornet*, as the OPAS called its base utility motorboat, to transport him to town, leaving the man alone for a few moments. Burton ran back to the dock just in time to see him get up and race into the bush, abandoning the sacking and bandages. The so-called accident victim had wanted only a ride to civilization and he got it.

The introduction of H-boats greatly hastened the ability of forest surveyors to cover more territory. Timber stand surveys by hardy bushmen on foot with cumbersome measuring chains, as the heavy tapes were called, was time-consuming work. The OPAS had proven an airplane covered more country in a week than a team of men could inventory in a whole season.

Burton often took ground parties into the wilderness, waited until they selected their random wood samples, then returned them to base. With identification completed in the field, observers settled into the H-boats' cramped front cockpit and finished the count aloft. Wind-burned, watery-eyed and half frozen, they quickly learned how to read tree characteristics and values from high altitudes. Jackpine, they said, appeared blurry and spruce trees looked dark and pinlike when viewed straight down. Budworm devastation changed the lush forests to dry, flame red tracts ready to ignite in the first lightning storm.

With nothing to obstruct their arm movement nor any form of intercom between the cockpits, observers signaled by hand and expected the pilot to turn to the appropriate compass heading. At midday, they landed at one of twelve strategically located refueling stations beside the railway tracks. On warm days, the crew found themselves roaring at full power to the end of the lake only to be unable to take off. In such cases, Burton closed the throttle, shut down the cantankerous Liberty and waited for the afternoon heat to dissipate. Once airborne, turbulence sometimes prevented legible sketching. There was nothing to do except to turn for home and endure the odors of hot oil, sagging fabric and water-rotted wood wafting into their nostrils another day.

At seaplane bases, life was never dull. When fog, high winds or rain stopped all flying, pilots gathered together to pass the time. On one occasion, Burton returned to base after a side trip in the *Green Hornet* to Sioux Lookout for mail. In the pouch, he discovered a thick, official-looking envelope addressed to Schiller and bearing the imposing black lettering of a lawyer's logo. He handed it over to the famous pilot who immediately ripped it open.

Inside were two large checks from a New York legal firm, one for Schiller and the other for mechanic Al Cheesman. Schiller, a natural raconteur, launched into the story of how the checks found him in Sioux Lookout. The men relaxed and listened on their boxes and crates in the warmth of the humid office a few yards from a pair of tethered H-boats.

Before signing on with the OPAS, Schiller and Cheesman bootlegged whisky from New York harbor. Using a decrepit war surplus HS-2L, they flew to ships anchored beyond the legal three mile limit and returned with loads of illicit liquor. Out of sight of land, they touched down at prearranged locations to rendezvous with customers. On one trip, the well-worn Liberty engine, which rarely exceeded 100 hours before overhaul, threatened to die prematurely. Backfiring and losing altitude, they barely staggered back to safety.

To their dismay, they had been seen by a revenue boat which came dashing up to make an arrest. Cheesman and Schiller, however, frantically jettisoned all their valuable cargo into the Atlantic. In spite of a lack of incriminating evidence, an over-anxious New York paper ran the headline: "Schiller and Cheesman Caught Bootlegging with Aeroplane on New York Harbor."

The guilty pair, eager to recoup their losses, contacted a lawyer who specialized in libel and slander.

"Look," Schiller snapped, "See what they printed about us, defaming our fair names."

"Is there anything to it?" the lawyer asked. "Is it true?"

"Of course it's true," replied Schiller. "But they can't prove it."

"That's all I need to know," the lawyer said. "A clear case of defamation of character."

Cheesman and Schiller won the case and their pals at the Sioux Lookout base shared in the party brought about by the out-of-court settlement.

Airplanes routinely left Sioux Lookout and did not return for several days because of mechanical failures. Aircrew carried plenty of rations as part of their kits and could live for days on items like flour, lard, "sowbelly" (bacon), powdered milk and oatmeal. They also counted on catching or trapping fish and game to supplement their diets.

There were times when poor weather kept them stranded for more than a week. Although some H-boats carried experimental wireless, communication ceased once they disappeared beyond the horizon. As a result, Burton became involved in a rescue flight that would affect him for the rest of his life.

Schiller, dispatched on fire patrol out of Sioux Lookout on August 16, 1924, did not return at his scheduled time. Such flights, even with full gasoline tanks, could not stay aloft for more than four hours. When no word came on Schiller's location,

Burton was taken from his regular duties and assigned a search route southeast of the base toward Port Arthur.

With junior pilot Kenneth McBride and forestry observer Richard Gilbert aboard G-CAOC, Burton left Sioux Lookout. En route to a gasoline cache at Savanne on the CPR line where they would overnight, the crew studied every shoreline on both sides of their search corridor. In spite of the evening hour when air generally became smooth, turbulence from a fast-moving weather front made the ponderous H-boat difficult to handle as gusts kicked up plumes of spray from the waterways below.

As the huge aircraft followed the CPR tracks, they flew over a small section house. After a mile, they banked right toward an abandoned sawmill site which served as a seaplane dock and gasoline cache for the OPAS. Barely under control and his arms weakened from wrestling with the tottering H-boat, Burton banked left twice more over Lac des Milles Lac as two boys watched from the section house roof. One was fifteen-year-old Onni Saline who later became a successful hydraulic maintenance engineer. The horrified teenagers saw the H-boat's nose drop almost vertically during a turn.

Desperately, Burton pulled back the control wheel as the wings began rolling toward the vertical. With pain searing deep into his shoulders and arms, he nearly had the plummeting craft under control but could not stop it from slamming steeply into the forest floor. Splintered trees, shredded fabric and scattered pieces of struts marked the earth-shaking point of impact as wings folded forward and the engine ripped from its mounts. The crash had occurred a quarter mile from the nearest lakeshore.

Mechanic Lawrence Hemphill, who had been standing by with fuel drums opened, also witnessed the crash and rushed to telephone the Sioux Lookout base. Residents of Savanne, including Saline, scrambled into canoes and boats and pushed away from shore toward the crash site. Another H-boat flown by Pat Moloney and George Phillips soon arrived and landed at the cache just before dark.

With remaining daylight measured in minutes, rescue parties would waste time flailing around with dim lanterns trying to locate the wreckage. Phillips suggested that Moloney take off again and pinpoint the exact site. They quickly found the downed airplane and circled as Phillips blinked a flashlight to guide the land party.

By the time they reached the wreckage, four hours had elapsed. The searchers found the airplane with its tail standing vertically against the trees and broken wires tangled in the crushed branches. Burton lay drenched in gasoline with the white of a bone protruding from his left leg. McBride and Gilbert were unconscious.

Moved by boat to the railway line, the rescuers transferred the three men to a Port Arthur-bound train. Before they could reach the city, McBride and Gilbert died. Three days later, a newspaper reported that Burton had a "restful night." When informed of the "...deaths of his machine companions, he was greatly disturbed."

The OPAS did not hold Burton responsible. The tragedy, experts said, was due to the flying boat's unstable handling characteristics in rough air.

"It was truly a regrettable accident, the more so because the season is rapidly drawing to a close and also because it was the first accident in 1,800 flying hours which the planes in service have completed this year," said OPAS director Roy Maxwell. As it happened, Schiller and Cheesman were slaking their thirst at a small hotel in the same region. Neither had any idea that a search was taking plce.

Burton never again flew a Curtiss HS-2L. His injuries necessitated the use of a cane for many years, and in later life his stiff leg and frequent pain were permanent reminders of the accident. Ed Burton, however, did not intend to let the incident put an end to his career.

During his lengthy convalescence, the aviation industry took root everywhere and northern air transportation had its true beginnings. While bed-ridden or confined to short walks, Burton read about the gold strikes in Red Lake, Ontario, which called for Curtiss HS-2Ls to move men and equipment into the bush country. Soon, entrepreneurs and former OPAS acquaintances created air services and bought airplanes and hired pilots. For a long time Burton, much to his regret, could only watch from the sidelines.

CHAPTER THREE

Passenger Hopping and Seeking Ships

For OPAS pilots in the 1920s, no medical assistance or unemployment insurance existed. Maxwell, concerned for the welfare of his staff, arranged to keep Burton on partial pay. Eventually, Burton talked his way into a position as an agent for Western Canada Airways (WCA). The company, formed on December 10, 1926, was owned by ex-fighter pilot H. A. "Doc" Oaks and Winnipeg businessman James A. Richardson.

Burton managed the office in Hudson, twelve miles by rail west of Sioux Lookout. When not invoicing, meeting payrolls or dispatching, he ran a motor launch from WCA's dock to a sheltered bay where Oaks anchored a pair of Fokker Universal seaplanes.

By July, 1927, Burton's leg pain was becoming almost unbearable and he switched frequently from cane to crutches. Each day, he walked a little further to exercise the limb and managed to keep up with whatever work Oaks assigned. Finally, frustrated by the endless pain, he decided to go to England to see if British doctors could do more.

While on leave of absence at the Burton family home in Redhill, a letter arrived, tersely advising him that the agent's position with WCA would be unavailable on his return. Oaks had surreptitiously informed the Winnipeg head office that the Hudson base had been left in a "chaotic state." Flabbergasted that his friend and fellow pilot would "stab him in the back," Burton would not permit the matter to cast a shadow over his future. He immediately fired off a vitriolic letter to Oaks.

"Far from being in a chaotic state, my work in general was kept strictly up to date in spite of quantities of unnecessary correspondence with the Winnipeg office and of the fact that my office was used as a general meeting place for the whole staff, there being no other accommodation for them at that time," he wrote.

To add to the disorder, equipment and spares had arrived at Hudson after Burton's departure. In spite of repeated requests before his leave, WCA did not provide enough invoices and office staff to handle the paperwork associated with supplying mining communities. Since John E. Hammell began developing gold claims discovered by Lorne and Ray Howey on July 25, 1925, near Red Lake, exploration companies and prospectors inundated the bush country north of Hudson.

"No effort was spared by me to create good will with our customers by the prompt forwarding of their mail and express, and strict attention to correspondence and personal favors, though my efforts were entirely counteracted by the apparent lack of courtesy shown in letters sent from the head office...." slammed Burton.

Ironically, Oaks acknowledged Burton's conscientious work and shifted the blame to another dismissed employee. Nevertheless, and in spite of a favorable letter of recommendation, WCA did not rehire Burton. He never forgave his former friend for blemishing his reputation in the bush flying community.

Years later, when Oaks campaigned for political office in the Port Arthur riding, he met Burton at a general store in the village of MacDiarmid, north of Nipigon. Burton, who had developed tremendous upper body strength to compensate for his leg injuries, pounced on his ex-friend. The resulting battle left the two former friends badly bruised and embarrassed.

Burton remained in England until December, 1927, before returning to Canada by ship. The British physicians had not been able to improve on the work of the Canadian doctors. He would still need a cane whenever the pain became overwhelming. During the return journey, he met twenty-four-year-old Emma Lucille Tervin from St. Augustine, Florida. Immediately attracted to each other, they vowed to keep in touch after the vessel docked at New York. "Cile," as Burton called the young newspaper reporter, returned to St. Augustine and Burton boarded a train to Toronto.

When his injuries had healed enough to enable him to renew his pilot's license, Burton looked for flying work. A few months before, the greatest boost aviation had ever known took place when Charles Lindbergh's *Spirit of St. Louis* landed safely in France. The following year, Canadians were electrified when the *Bremen*, a Junkers W 33, left Ireland with three men aboard. Thirty-seven hours later, they landed at Greenly Island in the Strait of Belle Isle and broke their undercarriage. Burton's old friend, Duke Schiller, made headlines for his part in the rescue flight.

Inspired by all the exciting news, Burton attended an instructor refresher course at the RCAF's Camp Borden. On April 10, 1928, he climbed into a delightful biplane called a de Havilland DH60X Moth registered G-CAKE. After an hour of dual training in an airplane he had never flown before, Burton flew solo. Exhilarated to be aloft and in control—the first time since the H-boat crash—he floated above the panorama of southern Ontario's greenery and toward the vast expanse of Lake Simcoe, east of the camp. Finally, his instructor signaled him down and they began the serious business of refining Burton's teaching skills.

"We were doing two flights a day in that nice little Moth until at last, somebody figured I'd be able to get through the rigid flight tests they'd developed," said Burton. "On the second of June, the CO, Squadron Leader G. S. Brookes, took me up in another Moth and ran me through a review and that was it."

As public interest continued growing and hundreds discovered the new world in the skies, demand for pilots increased while the pool of war surplus veterans dwindled. Canada's Department of National Defence (DND) had developed an assistance program in which any interested community could engage an instructor and air engineer to staff a licensed flying field. Furthermore, each pupil qualifying for a private pilot license received $100. Enthusiasm throughout Canada surpassed all expectations and the program led to openings for instructors.

The Toronto Flying Club became one of the DND recipients, and two weeks after Burton passed his tests with Brookes, he found work at Leaside, one of his former training fields. He and ex-OPAS/RFC pilot Carter Guest began instructing people from all walks of life. Unlike his Jenny days, Burton had to be patient and often wondered at the inability of some students to grasp the basics. No one could be rushed—they were paying customers and, he reminded himself, there was no war on.

When not aloft in Canadian-built Moths G-CAKR and G-CAKS, Burton and Guest lectured constantly on theory of flight, airmanship, aero engines and airframes. During one of these sessions, Burton happened to look through the classroom window and noticed mechanic William Boucher siphoning gasoline from a drum. Since the gas came too slowly for his liking, Boucher put the rubber hose into his mouth, sealed his lips around it and inhaled deeply.

The effect of a sudden torrent of gasoline down his throat caused Boucher to lose consciousness. Guest and Burton rushed over and pulled him away from the drum. After several rounds of artificial resuscitation, the dazed mechanic sat up, spluttered and looked around.

"Nice going, Billy, old boy," laughed Guest, slapping the muddled mechanic on the back. "Now, how about telling us how many miles you can get to the gallon?"

Flying instruction during the formative years of organizations like the Toronto Flying Club was a highly respected profession. The clique of those who flew and taught others to fly was a small one. Men like Burton knew their colleagues through cross country flights and fly-ins at a time when aviation recognized no borders. A colorful example of cooperation took place on April 10, 1929, when the Toronto Flying club reciprocated a visit by the United States Army Air Corps First Pursuit Squadron to the Canadian National Exhibition the previous year.

Organized by Burton and Guest, twenty-nine club members arrived at muddy Leaside and prepared a peacetime civil squadron of de Havilland Moths and two five-seat biplanes called Buhl Air Sedans. With military precision, ground handlers hauled each airplane into line for photographers of the Toronto Telegram, and designated helpers in white coveralls spun the propellers by hand. The sound of a dozen engines shook the citizens of Leaside. At 12:05 P.M., the first Moth rolled down the grass flying field and eased into the air.

"One by one or sometimes in pairs, we all got off and headed south toward Toronto," said Burton. "We flew in formation across the city, turned parallel to the lake (Ontario) and then paralleled the north side of Lake Erie on what the press called Ontario's first international good-will flight to the States."

After two hours and forty minutes, warmed only by the engine's oily heat blasting by in the slipstream, the fleet landed at Selfridge Field near Detroit, Michigan. When celebrations ended with a generous display of American hospitality, not enough daylight remained for a return to Toronto. The group decided to stay overnight.

Next day, the Canadians entertained their hosts with formation flying over the city before crossing the Detroit River into Ontario. Pushed along by a tailwind in a sky bereft of "serious air pockets" as a Toronto Star reporter/passenger called the jolts he felt the previous day, they landed in Leaside two hours and five minutes after takeoff. The ensuing media publicity encouraged more and more Torontonians to make the short drive to Leaside for airplane rides and flying lessons.

An ambitious team, Burton and Guest believed proper exposure could entice more students and promoted what became known as "general aviation." The public had become captivated by dramatic Atlantic crossings and air races as aviation magazines now appeared on newsstands everywhere. Soon, more Canadians could understand the differences between a gigantic Ford Trimotor transport and the tiny Taylor Brothers Chummy, forerunner of the ubiquitous Piper Cub series.

Following months of incident-free teaching and testing Moths, Burton and Guest used club airplanes to participate in the First Annual Essex County Air Derby at Windsor. With student pilot E. Machelle to defray costs, Burton flew Moth G-CAKR. Acquired new on May 5, 1928, and powered by the 85-hp Cirrus engine, the airplane should have provided a trouble-free trip to Windsor. Before the race ended, Burton and Machelle would acquire more experience than they bargained for.

"We started out into a headwind and a couple hours later, the engine stopped dead a little west of London," Burton said. "We got down without breaking anything, did a quick fix and got right back to the race."

Burton had little to do for the first hour but relax and allow Machelle to fly. As he settled into the seat, he reflected on the slow, horse-drawn wagons and underpowered automobiles crawling along back roads west of London. Tiny dots of cattle and flame red barns sometimes caught his eye. Suddenly, without a splutter or kick, the engine stopped again.

"Down we went for a field that looked fairly smooth," said Burton. "It was, and we got away without hurting the poor little Moth and again tinkered around and we took off and got into Windsor."

At Windsor, no one could find anything wrong with G-CAKR. On the return, another stoppage put them into a recently mowed tobacco field near Chatham. After a thorough full power run-up, the Cirrus seemed to run well but Burton kept a wary eye as they approached the more populated areas. Sure enough, their mettle was tested again with another engine failure near Brantford. By the time G-CAKR limped to Leaside, the two pilots knew they had lost the race. However, the trip was not a waste of time since they profited from plenty of forced landing practice.

Hijackings, bomb-carrying maniacs and security checks were unknown in a period when flying organizations did everything possible to develop a receptive public. As student enrolment increased, teaching duties took most of the instructors' time. Charter work also expanded when businessmen discovered that Moths could land in almost any open field adjoining major cities. These extra revenue trips at flying clubs were welcomed and sometimes, they carried a measure of drama.

Allan Brown, an instructor at the London Flying Club, told Burton of his experience with a charter customer who explained that he had two pressing appointments. The first was in London and the second involved a meeting in Toronto, ninety-three miles northeast. The airplane would enable him to keep both of his rendezvous.

"About three in the afternoon, right after the passenger's London appointment, he shows up at the hangar, rushes in and puts on a flying suit Al gave him," said Burton. "The club mechanics had already warmed up the Moth so they took off for Toronto."

A few moments after the Moth departed, a posse of police cars with flashing lights and blaring sirens slid to a halt at the London flying field. Car doors slammed and blue-uniformed policemen demanded to know the whereabouts of Brown's passenger. Mechanic Charles Smith pointed to the airplane's slowly fading silhouette. The customer turned out to be a notorious bank robber who had just held up a London bank. Club members became concerned for Brown when police told them the man carried a gun.

As the tiny biplane neared the outskirts of Toronto, the passenger politely asked through the speaking tube if Brown could find somewhere besides Leaside to drop him. The cab ride into the heart of the city would be expensive and too far from his second appointment. Anxious to promote repeat business, Brown landed at Barker's Field beside Dufferin Street. The man paid in cash, thanked Brown for the quick, pleasant journey and disappeared across the road. In his hand, he carried a large black suitcase.

With time to spare, Brown decided to hop across to Leaside to visit Burton. Minutes after swinging around and shutting down, a swarm of policemen surrounded the airplane. When they discovered the empty passenger seat, they demanded to know what happened to the passenger. Brown, shocked to learn that his gentleman client was a dangerous criminal, explained about the unplanned landing at Barker's Field.

Several police cars dashed to Dufferin Street. The remaining officers held Brown and questioned him for hours. They could not understand how he unknowingly cooperated with a criminal without being an accomplice. They never caught the robber with the suitcase, but Canada's first aerial getaway made interesting news and drew more attention to the Toronto Flying Club. The episode might have had a different ending if the airplane had been equipped with radio, but such innovations did not become standard until years later.

In the spring of 1929, a Buhl CA-5 Air Sedan registered NC1771 appeared at Leaside. Burton took the controls of the strange-looking American-built airplane for a demonstration flight and was impressed with its performance and size. Eventually, National Air Transport at Barker's Field acquired a Buhl registered G-CATO. Powered by a 200-hp Wright J-5 Whirlwind engine, the CA-5 had been designed in 1927 at Marysville, Michigan, near Sarnia, Ontario.

A fabric-covered biplane with enclosed cabin, the Buhl had established an impressive record during the 1927 Dole Derby Race to Hawaii. One called *Miss Doran* lurched airborne with 2,400 pounds of gasoline and three people—remarkable considering the gross weight of over 5,000 pounds supported by only 350 square feet of lifting surface. This well publicized event and the sight of National Air Transport's G-CATO tempted Burton to consider switching employers.

Of an adventurous frame of mind and not tempted greatly by positions that were secure as opposed to interesting, he considered his options. At the time, Lindbergh had proven that air transport had come of age and was to be taken seriously.

Tulley and Metcalfe, two ex-OPAS pilots, made an attempt on the Atlantic but after they left from Harbour Grace, Newfoundland, were never heard from again. A plan by members of the Toronto Flying Club for a similar crossing was called off when too many large investors wanted to ride the Fokker across the ocean.

Burton's last flight with the Toronto Flying Club took place on April 15, 1929. Two weeks later, he began flying with National Air Transport Ltd. which operated de Havilland Moths as well as two Buhl Air Sedans. Before long, work took an exciting turn when a call came in from the *Toronto Telegram*. The aviation-oriented newspaper needed a Moth quickly for reporter Kim Beattie.

On Saturday morning, May 4, 1929, agents at Canada Steamship Lines were worried about their freighter *Saskatoon* after gale force winds ravaged Lake Ontario. A tip to the *Telegram* hinted that a disaster might have taken place. No one knew whether the vessel had gone down or was nestled safely in a cove out of contact with the shipping world. National Air Transport turned to its newest pilot.

"They gave me G-CATF, a little de Havilland Moth, so I went out and made sure it carried every drop of fuel possible and the oil was topped up before putting Beattie in," said Burton. "Although it was still pretty early, the wind was already rocking the wings at fifteen miles an hour."

Burton and Beattie took off with no idea how long the search for the missing freighter would last. As they flew over the sands of the Scarboro Bluffs, raging waves slamming into the beaches could not have made either man feel at ease. In Burton's case, his stiffened leg eliminated any chance of swimming to safety if the engine quit.

"Lake Ontario's shoreline looked like a white run of foam and for a mile out from land, the water had turned to a dirty brown from the stirred bottom," reported Beattie. "Beyond, the water was green, the merging of the sky and lake indistinct, lost in a blur of grey mists. Following the shore, the strong tail wind sent the Moth scudding swiftly eastbound with a retarded throttle."

Burton overflew deserted beaches, flooded banks and debris-covered water but saw nothing resembling a ship. He continued east to Port Hope until black sky to the north threatened to push the rocking Moth far from shore. Beattie, spotting a lighthouse in the distance, thought at first it could be the missing vessel. Seconds later, he realized he had been tricked by gigantic white breakers slamming against the stone reefs.

A little later, Burton noticed the faint outline of a freighter low in the water and far offshore. In spite of the risk—only a few weeks before, he experienced four engine failures in one day—he banked toward it only to discover that a wide wake and belch of flattened black smoke showed the vessel was not under duress but steaming safely westward.

Near Wellington Bay off the Kingston-Toronto shipping route, Burton's keen eyes picked out another vessel. It too chugged west without difficulty. Soon, close to Timber Island, he came across what appeared to be "two long dark logs."

"So we had to figure out if one of them was the *Saskatoon*. There was nothing to do except throttle back and go down and look," said Burton. "We went low enough that spray from the rollers splattered the windscreen and the turbulence shook the wings so hard we could hardly focus. People were lining the rails of both ships and waving like crazy by the time we got close enough to see the names painted on the front."

Beattie marked the ships as the *Norman P. Clement* and *Reynder*. They continued east, still hoping they would find the *Saskatoon* on the surface instead of the bottom of Lake Ontario.

With G-CATF's fuel supply dropping, Burton decided to land at the nearest available flying field. Tracking slightly north across Prince Edward County, he flew over territory he recognized from his cadet days. Gliding across the boiling Bay of Quinte, he touched down at Deseronto after two hours of shaking and holding the controls with sweat-soaked hands.

While topping off the Moth's tank, Beattie telephoned the Telegram in Toronto and learned that the missing freighter had turned back under tow to Kingston. By the time they were ready to take off for Barker's Field, surface winds were ripping across the old aerodrome at forty-five miles per hour.

Although there had not been a spectacular, headline-grabbing ship sinking, Beattie had to have his story and photos filed as quickly as possible. Burton knew the tipsy Moth could handle the wind and eased the throttle forward. In seconds, the little airplane seemed to levitate in the brief ground run before climbing above the countryside. Two hours and ten minutes later, they stepped out of the dusty cockpit onto the grass at Barker's Field.

Back at his downtown desk, Beattie waxed enthusiastic about the tremendous area covered on the short trip. Best of all, he had been away from Toronto for only six and a half hours and returned with an exciting story. On May 6, 1929, the evening edition ran the headline:

"Telegram Plane Roars Over Wild Lake, Seeking Ships, Reporting Those in Shelter"

"The flight itself demonstrated one of the great methods of rescue the aeroplane will be in the future in time of disaster on the Canadian lakes," wrote Beattie.

Interviewed several times, the thirty-eight-year-old, leather-helmeted Burton became a hero after a newspaper drawing depicted "Ed Burton—National Air Transport." His serious visage flanked characters flying an unlikely low-winged airplane on forest fire patrol. Another rendering showed a student tossing Burton's cane overboard while Burton, the instructor, swore frantically; the cane represented the airplane's control stick.

Pilots at National Air Transport sold hundreds of rides at a time when Canadians were beginning to appreciate what *Aero Digest* May, 1928, had called, "...the game for men with sporting blood." The company sent its airplanes far afield in an organized manner to exhibitions and fairs. The quick trip over the family farm became an important staple for National Air Transport. Besides the single-passenger Moths, the company had an advantage over competitors because of the four-passenger Buhls.

On one grueling session, Burton took off and landed twenty-five times in Moth G-CATF from a field near Goderich. At another three-day open air fair, he logged forty-five hops and then flew to Windsor for thirty-six more. During one period, he arrived at Windsor's Walker Airport on May 8 and left seventeen days later after nonstop sightsee trips along the St. Clair River. Americans and Canadians wanted to brag that they had flown with one wing in Canada and the other in the United States.

"I had one particular trip that stood out as different from the run-of-the-mill joy hops," Burton said. "The *Telegram* hired me again and this time, we weren't doing any flying over open water looking for sinking ships. My passenger—a photographer—had been assigned to take pictures of ladies in swim suits at a fashion show."

Burton enjoyed meeting the public and sharing his enthusiasm with anyone who ventured out to cow pastures or exhibition grounds. Although the work was never dull, growth of the company seemed unlikely. His chance meeting with ex-OPAS pilot Leigh Brintnell, Western Canada Airways manager, gave rise to hopes that he might be rehired. In response to a query sent to Winnipeg on August 13, 1929, Brintnell had replied that no vacancies existed; however, the company was "expanding very fast."

As events turned out, Western Canada Airways secured more mail contracts than any Canadian organization and had, in fact, outbid National Air Transport. At the time, WCA's future looked promising. Nevertheless, no one predicted the stock market crash which later retarded the growth of the world's aviation industry.

Brintnell, true to his word, remembered his old friend as a conscientious, capable pilot and overlooked the messy office incident of 1927. Burton left National Air Transport on December 1, 1929, and accepted a posting to St. Hubert as a mail pilot with Western Canada Airways.

CHAPTER FOUR

Night or Storms—
The Mail Goes Through

With the start of the depression in October, 1929, Western Canada Airways' expansion continued. Exploration flights into the Yukon and throughout the Arctic were milestones leading to the airline's progress. A series of airmail contracts guaranteed revenue and became an important turning point in the company's fortunes. As a bonus, the federal government encouraged industry by establishing flying fields, building hangars and erecting acetylene light beacons for night navigation.

When Burton arrived at St. Hubert near Montreal, he entered a world far different from his first airmail flight of 1918. Instead of flimsy Jennies, a variety of sturdy airplanes added interest to the work. Almost all had high lift wings, carried four to seven passengers and were the workhorses in the development of Canadian aviation. Many, like the Fairchilds and Fokkers, were built in Canada under license. Others, such as the American Pitcairns, Stearmans and Travel Airs, had been carefully studied before selection for purchase in the United States.

These aircraft moved mail every day to Quebec City and Rimouski and reached out across the forests of New Brunswick and Maine to Saint John and Moncton. Westward, they flew as far as Detroit's Wayne County Airport in Michigan. Each Saturday, despatchers posted weekly schedules which sometimes required pilots to be on duty as early as three in the morning.

"We seldom knew which airplane we'd be given until just before the trip," Burton said. "As the airports didn't have hard-surfaced runways, most were equipped with large, low pressure donut tires designed to mushroom out on soft ground. A few still used tail skids since tail wheels and brakes hadn't come into common use yet."

On December 6, 1929, Burton dispatched himself on a familiarization flight in a Fairchild 71 registered CF-ACY. Built by Fairchild Aircraft Ltd. in Montreal, it used a 330-hp Pratt & Whitney radial engine and became part of a family of airplanes which played leading roles in the opening of Canada's northland. Its boxlike interior made the "Seventy-One" an ideal mail carrier and Burton flew several. In later years, he singled out the Fairchild 71 as one of the best all-purpose bush airplanes.

As the hours went into Burton's logbook, he adapted well to the airmail service. Long distances, muddy or snow-covered landing fields, treacherous weather systems and rudimentary navigation aids made the job hazardous; in a five-month period, five mailplanes crashed. As a safety measure, aviation inspector G. G. Wakeman proposed utilizing ground signals with white canvas strips. A square set out by a station agent suggested the pilot could continue into good weather. A cross suggested turning back.

"The real problem was, the nice little canvas strips only indicated weather conditions at our next destination," said Burton. "Without radio—they were too heavy to carry around in those days—we had no idea about changes along the way or if fog or smoke would stop us from getting down once we got there. None of us liked finding a place socked in with the airplane almost out of gas and nowhere to go."

Burton's initial months exposed him to more blizzards, deep snow, fog and ice than he had ever experienced. Unlike passenger hopping, he could not cancel for the day. The post office demanded that the mail must go through.

Pilots pushed on and "...letters take wings. Nowhere is it more assiduously lived up to than by the men who fly His Majesty's mails in flimsy, roaring craft of fabric and metal," wrote a *Toronto Evening Telegram* reporter. Slowly, such fatalistic attitudes disappeared from the aviation industry to be replaced by higher regards for safety.

Once, a sudden snowstorm forced Burton into a diagonal landing across unseen railroad tracks. After an hour waiting for weather to improve, he skipped along the ties into the air and carried on. On another occasion, he had the dubious honor of being part of the reason for the first interruption of the Saint John-Moncton-Quebec aerial postal service an hour after leaving Moncton.

"Unable to continue with clouds of mist blotting out his course over the frozen surface of the river, pilot E. C. Burton this morning glided the air mail machine to a landing on the ice of the Saint John near the Hermitage," spouted a Fredericton newspaper on December 14, 1929. "The landing was not entirely without mishap, one of the skis of the plane being damaged in the forced descent." In fact, explained Ted Burton years later, his father told him the broken ski had penetrated the cabin but no one was hurt.

When deteriorating weather reached a point where venturing into it was foolhardy, pilots amused themselves any way they could. Burton, when compelled to tie down his airplane away from base, studied the area for potential emergency landing sites. When poor conditions persisted, he sketched his surroundings and, in time, became an excellent artist with a talent for detail. His artistic mind also delved into poetry, none of which he ever disclosed to his peers. One brief ditty turned up between the pages of his dog-eared journals years later:

A pilot is a guy
Who bums for an existence
He waits until the fog blows by
And sits and idly wonders why
The weather will not let him fly
So he can make subsistence.

Western Canada Airways' (the name changed to Canadian Airways after the original WCA and the Aviation Corporation of Canada incorporated on June 27, 1930) longest mail run took place from Montreal to Sherbrooke to Megantic and across Maine via Greenville to Saint John and Moncton. The uninhabited conifer and deciduous forest was breathtakingly beautiful especially during low-level fall flights, but navigation demanded special attention.

Pilots learned to recognize the profile of Mount Katahdin towering above the surrounding hills. Burton had been told that surveyors discovered Mount Katahdin to be ten feet short of a mile in height. A dedicated group of patriotic boosters erected a ten-foot cairn so they could boast of Maine's mile-high mountain.

On a familiarization flight, Burton took off with newly transferred pilot W. "Babe" Woollett in a de Havilland 80A Puss Moth registered CF-AVG. In the enclosed cabin, Burton rode in front with Woollett behind. With no speaking tube system or intercom, they shouted over the Gipsy Major engine to communicate.

Burton, Woollett recalled, had an open, friendly manner of asking: "What do you think?" As weather worsened along "the bloody Khyber Pass," Woollett became anxious. Whenever Burton turned to speak, he relaxed on the controls and the Puss Moth dropped closer to the ground. Much to Woollett's relief, they managed a low-level reverse turn without clipping trees and returned to St. Hubert for another try.

Later, Burton related Woollett's experience over Maine in a Fairchild FC2 with mechanic Al Parker. With no warning or gradual loss of power, the engine suddenly stopped dead at 4,000 feet.

"Looks like we have to go down," Woollett said in the silence.

"About the only thing we can do," Parker agreed. "What goes up has to come down."

And down they came.

Woollett selected a stand of seventy-foot poplars near a railroad line. During the glide, Parker stretched out on the Fairchild's floor and braced himself with a sleeping bag while Woollett tightened his seat belt. Wings snapped off and slammed backward, canvas ripped, metal bent and wires twanged as the wreckage plunged through the trees. Unhurt, they unloaded and carried their two mail bags to the railway and waited for a train.

During one of Burton's Toronto-bound trips with Fokker Super Universal CF-AJF, heavy fog blotted out the landmarks. Lowering ceilings left him little choice except to find a landing area quickly. Desperate, he searched for open ground and wheeled the Fokker around. A gigantic airplane for the time, it was not designed for short field work.

"There wasn't much in the way of big enough fields to put the Fokker down in but finally, a little pasture that didn't have cattle running all over it showed up under the nose," recalled Burton. "Somehow, the airplane fit, but as far as I was concerned, the only reason I got into that little hole was because of the landing practice from those hundreds of passenger hops back with National Air Transport."

After turning over the mail to the local postmaster, he called Canadian Airways superintendent "Peggy" Ingram in Montreal to report.

"We just got word that one of our airplanes between Montreal and Toronto had cracked up and both occupants were killed," Ingram said. "We were waiting to see if it was you."

Burton knew mail carrying could be a dangerous profession. He had constant reminders—detours around thunderstorms, broken rocker exhausts on dark nights, and several "engine quit dead" entries in his logbook. The work paid well—senior pilots earned $5,000 per year—but Burton knew that incidents and accidents could happen to the most experienced. This was made clear when he was asked to fly over the south side of the St. Lawrence en route to Rimouski.

At the outskirts of a tiny French-Canadian village, he spotted a long line of cars in a funeral procession. Company officials wanted Burton to circle the cemetery several times. The man in the casket was Herve Simoneau, the pilot killed the same day Burton had wrestled his ungainly Fokker Universal into the tiny field. As he dropped a wreath, he looked down on the grieving group and wondered why one was taken and others survived.

In the midst of a dangerous lifestyle portrayed by reporter Kim Beattie as endless thrills, risky blind landings and "gaspy" takeoffs into jet black walls of night, Burton never waned in his correspondence with Lucille Tervin. Near Christmas, 1929, he boarded a southbound train at Montreal's Windsor Station and remained on it until Florida's orange groves replaced the leafless trees of Canadian winter.

On January 3, 1930, a newspaper reported a marriage in Daytona Beach Presbyterian Church: English teacher Miss Lucille Tervin, "striking in a spring outfit of maroon, especially becoming to her brunette type," married "...the pilot and well-known businessman of Toronto." The gushy report, however, was not accurate. No one knew the pilot as a businessman and the bride had long ago forsaken teaching to pursue journalism. At the end of a honeymoon to Georgia and Ohio, they returned to Montreal.

As the 1930 navigation season opened on the St. Lawrence, Burton flew numerous runs to Rimouski. From this riverside community, the tug boat *Jolibert* met trans-Atlantic ships like the *Duchess of Atholl, Empress of Australia* or *Empress of France*. These gigantic ocean liners contacted ground stations from 200 miles away and stopped at Father Point to transfer mail. The time saved was significant since the liners would not dock again for three days. Airplanes, connecting early with incoming vessels from Europe, were able to deliver the Royal Mail to Montreal before the ships had arrived at Quebec City.

Sometimes the extensive preparations and precautions for speedy pick-up and delivery were to no avail and frustrated the most experienced pilots. To pass the hours spent waiting for safer weather, Burton became acquainted with the local French-Canadian population, as he described to Lucille:

Juillet 17, 1930
Hotel St-Laurent
Rimouski, Quebec

...After supper I drove out to St. Anaclet with Mr. Caron and four other men to a political meeting. The conservatives were holding forth from one balcony and the liberals from another. The mob surged to and fro—threatening to fight but it did not get further than noise and gesticulations.

I was introduced to one wild-looking man as follows—"This is ze man what fly from Montreal yesterday in two hours ten minute—he fly one hundred thousand feet high in ze hair." "My my," said the wild-looking man. "You are not scared to fly so high—Huhh!!?..."

On May 26, Burton battled heavy rain from Ottawa to Montreal to pick up one passenger and 700 pounds of mail for a 274-mile northeast run to Rimouski. After overnighting, the skies

Sketched while laying over in Montreal. A vignette of small town life in Quebec.

cleared for what he expected would be a pleasant homeward journey with a stop at Quebec City.

"We left Rimouski yesterday morning in beautiful weather but ran into fog toward Quebec so turned back and landed near St. Anne," he wrote to Lucille from a Ste. Anne de la Pocatiere hotel, sixty-five miles downriver from Quebec City. "We had lunch and got a report on the weather and took off again later but ran into very low clouds within a few miles of Quebec and had to turn back again, landing in the same field. There is a strong east wind and I cannot get away before tomorrow at earliest as the rain is pouring down and the clouds are low."

Some flights took place between Ottawa and St. Hubert. These runs terminated in the capital city where mail pilots basked in the expense-paid luxury of the Chateau Laurier Hotel. After a pleasant evening of wining and dining, they rushed back to St. Hubert in the early morning where the Toronto mail had already arrived. Carrying both Ottawa and Toronto mail, the pilots jumped into warmed up replacement airplanes and took off to meet the Jolibert at Rimouski.

Winter's whiteouts caused many terrifying moments but nothing matched the fury of rampaging thunderstorms on the St. Lawrence. After leaving St. Hubert, Burton noticed black skies and roiling, lightning-laced clouds to his left. Thinking he could beat the storm, he continued with an 800-pound load of mail. Past Quebec City, the mass of rising air and heavy rain crossed his path.

The laboring Fairchild 71 gained height rapidly in spite of the application of full nose down pressure on the control stick. Turbulence thundering against the thin fabric sides and the scream of wind forcing its way into the cockpit nearly deafened Burton. A horrifying smash and blinding blue glare across the windshield accompanied by odors of ozone made him think lightning had struck the wood-wing Fairchild.

Still upright, and barely in control of the wildly gyrating airplane, he ruddered south a few degrees at a time toward a patch of blue sky. Rain turned forward visibility into a river and hail clobbered the leading edges of the wings.

"This time it really looked like we wouldn't get out with an intact skin," he said later, characteristically understating the battle for his life. "The Fairchild was still going up no matter what I did. Down below, I could see we hadn't made any headway, then finally it was like somebody turning an electric switch; we came into that beautiful patch of sky and the air went calm at the tail end of the storm."

Burton had saved the Royal Mail and his own hide by unwittingly taking advantage of the poorly understood phenomenon of wind circulation around thunderstorm cells to find smooth air behind the storm. With upper winds at his back, he turned back on track for Rimouski.

However, the ordeal was not completely over. Fine misty rain lowered visibility and seemed to stretch out the weary miles until finally, Rimouski's tiny skyline appeared on the horizon. The mail went onward to the outgoing *Empress of Australia*. No one, except an exhausted air mail pilot, knew how close the mail bags had come to an untimely end.

The next day, Burton returned to St. Hubert. Cruising at low level, he saw crowds in the riverside communities surveying the storm's devastation. Everywhere, he counted roofs torn from barns and houses, exploded buildings and downed electric poles. In many cases, not even a frame remained; nothing except heaps of splintered wood and broken brick.

Years of looking down from cockpits made Burton highly observant. On some flights along the St. Lawrence River, he frequently encountered a pilot who was rumored to have been a German submarine commander during World War I. The man ostensibly used a Loening amphibian to chase rum runners on behalf of the Canadian government.

While stationed in St. Hubert, Burton disliked the German's overbearing attitude toward mechanics and Canadians in general. He left Canada prior to the outbreak of World War II with an intimate knowledge of the Canadian coastline. Many ships went down in the St. Lawrence and off the coast during the war years as a result of U-boat actions. It was said later that the German's maps had been put to good use by Nazi submarines to terrorize shipping.

In October, Burton accepted a transfer to Toronto to superintend mail flying from both sides of Ontario's capital. He, J. Smith and V. J. "Shorty" Hatton flew almost every airplane assigned to mail flying, including occasional flights in smaller Moth G-CAVH and Travel Air G-CAKU.

Canadian Airways mail routes seemed to survive, but the ripple effect of the stock market crash began eroding the air transportation industry. With less money, federal subsidization of eastern air mails was substantially reduced, and in many cases it was canceled completely.

"There had been considerable excitement in the city (Toronto) over the break in the stock exchange," wrote a worried Burton to Lucille in Montreal on October 29, 1930. "Several people who I know have had all their savings wiped out. Our savings were not affected as I had speculated only on a safe margin and hope to do well when the market recovers."

Canadian Airways believed in placing the most modern and practical airplanes on its mail runs. Night flying led the company to investigate the Stearman 4EM, later described as the "ultimate development of the civil biplane in North America" by historian Kenneth Molson. Even though the strong possibility existed that all mail contracts would be canceled, the first Stearman entered service on November 25, 1930.

Powered by a 420-hp Pratt & Whitney engine, the Junior Speedmail flew its maiden flight in Wichita, Kansas, less than a year before. The first two of these (CF-AMB and CF-AMC) to carry the company logo cost $17,797.25 each—a tremendous sum considering the economics of a time when an eight-cylinder luxury Hudson automobile cost $1,265 and butter averaged forty-five cents or less per pound in Northern Ontario.

During the first months, the air mail division found many faults with the Stearmans. This was not unusual for a new product, but some troubles exasperated management and defied all efforts of Canadian Airways' most experienced air engineers. Unreliable fuel quantity gauges caused what pilots called "pretty hairy times." Manager A. F. Ingram pointed out to factory representatives that the gauges would "...invariably go on the blink within a few days in spite of every attention."

"We didn't have much choice; times were tough and we started worrying about our jobs so we just put up with all these little problems," recalled Burton. "Sometimes, defective waterproof seals on the gas caps made the engine splutter anywhere near rain. The heaters hardly made cold weather flying bearable, and gas and oil lines leaked. Once we got down, the air engineers couldn't get at the inside because the factory didn't put enough inspection panels on."

Other problems included cracked gas tanks. One pilot went down in Maine after fuel leaked from an eight-inch split on the front section of the tank. Also, the Stearman's 134 miles per hour cruise speed necessitated protection from slipstream blast in the form of a canopy or larger windscreen.

Canadian Airways pilots felt duty-bound to keep the cargo dry and endure the cold. In response to Ingram's request for a waterproof hood, New York-based United Aircraft Exports Inc., Stearman distributors for North America, claimed that American pilots wanted, "...to be free to stick their head over the side, or pile out if necessary in an emergency without having to worry about removing impeding gadgets."

Of course, salesman S. A. McClellan added, "...there is never any question of having rain enter such a cockpit." In other words, no shelter from Canadian winters for Canadian pilots was in the cards.

It was during winter that Burton invented a version of the "no draft" window that enabled pilots to peer straight ahead through a horizontal slit in the glass. The angle of the upper glass deflected rain and wind without affecting visibility. Canadian Airways, however, did not adopt the modification. Later, the idea was adapted by the automobile industry.

As base superintendent, Burton ensured that staff received fair schedules and regular paychecks. Although he could have spent more time at desk duties, he preferred flying as often as possible. Many log entries showed "flight uneventful" but trips like a November 5, 1931, skirmish with sleet, low ceilings and night thunderstorms spoke volumes of the courage of the kind of men who pioneered Canada's airmail routes.

In this case, Burton fought his way down to a night landing in the rain-flecked glimmer of the Stearman's wing lights. Not content to slip into a hotel and sleep away the tension, he took a train to Detroit's Wayne County Airport with the mail bags slung over his shoulder.

During another night above Maine, snowstorms and strong winds forced him to fly with his wheels barely clearing the railroad tracks. Desperate to land, he squeezed his Stearman into a field so small he could not take off at daylight. Two men arrived by truck from St. Hubert, removed the wings and dismantled a nearby fence. Next, they pushed the ungainly biplane to a larger field so it could be flown back to St. Hubert.

Burton, described by Babe Woollett as a "jaunty Englishman," never encouraged the attention of the press. Dressed in flying helmet, goggles and calf-high boots, he was

I went out to the 'port to-day and

there was lots of snow in front of the hanger.

anything but the stereotyped, flamboyant airmail pilot favored by the media and filmmakers. Nevertheless, on December 19, 1931, he became involved in what one newspaper called a "...thrilling saga of the efforts of His Majesty's Royal Mail Service."

After a night departure from Toronto bound for Detroit with Stearman CF-AMC, he landed at Hamilton twenty minutes later, added another seventeen pounds and took off under a 2,500-foot ceiling.

Over London, he looked intently for a flare which would signal poor weather ahead. Seeing none, he flew on. At Tilbury, Burton spotted fog patches below but continued between layers to the southeast corner of Lake St. Clair. Unable to see the acetylene guidance beacons, he decided to return to Toronto and to wait for better conditions. As he settled into a homeward compass course, the mist condensed around him to form a solid wall.

To avoid losing all reference, he eased the throttle back and descended into the darkness.

"I came down as low as I dared in the hope of seeing lights beneath, when in the vicinity of Northwood saw a light directly underneath, too close for comfort with a glow around it from the fog," he said in a report to Canadian Airways. "So quickly pulled up and continued on my course."

By now, fuel shortage confirmed Burton's worst fears. The situation was made no easier by the fact that he had brought his wife and new son home from the hospital that same afternoon. Several indistinct blurs of lights appeared through the mist.

Fog closed in as the Stearman's main gas tank ran dry at 500 feet. He quickly clicked to a reserve tank and luckily, the reliable Pratt & Whitney restarted almost instantly. Back in business, he pointed the nose to where the last glimmers appeared and scrambled for altitude, watching the gas pressure gauge.

While Burton sought an improvement in flying conditions, worried airport officials in Detroit were broadcasting messages to all stations along the 217-mile route. Unsuspecting, Lucille waited for the customary telegram stating her husband had landed safely. As minutes ticked by and no message arrived, she became concerned. Although not a worrier, Lucille reminded herself that Canadian Airways had lost a mailplane a few weeks earlier.

In the blackness, his gravity tank went dry at 2,000 feet and the engine stopped. For the first time in his career, Burton, with his stiff leg a hindrance, would have to abandon an airplane in flight and dive into the darkness. Hidden danger from electric lines, sharp steeples or bone-chilling water could mean an agonizing end.

"I pulled one of the parachute flares, slipped off the safety belt, struggled out of the machine and took a header overboard, pulling the rip cord of the parachute as soon as I was clear," he said.

Burton drew a flashlight from the cavernous knee pocket of his Sidcot suit and shone the light on the parachute hoping that someone would see him. When tree branches flashed by forty feet above the ground, he knew he was close and jammed the light back into his pocket to prepare for landing. Until he saw the trees, he had not known whether the engine had stopped above land or Lake Erie.

Relieved to feel solid earth under his good leg, which had taken most of the touchdown shock, he smoked three cigarettes to pull himself together. With the parachute stuffed under his arm, he groped along in the silent, pitch black night to a fence, then found a gate. Finally a lane led him to a farm house.

"Where the hell did you come from?" was the truculent greeting from the farmer in whose field he had landed.

A newspaper reporter, taking literary license, described CF-AMC's last moments: "Like a meteor winging through the sky, Burton's mail aeroplane struck terror in the hearts of Lowbank (ten miles east of Dunnville) residents Saturday when they saw a great red flare drop from its bulk and then a terrific dive which climaxed in a dull thud when the machine crashed in the heart of the McCallum Swamp."

Two policemen and a postmaster located the wreckage less than a mile from where Burton landed. In spite of being told not to touch the gas-soaked remnants until daylight, they salvaged most of the cargo and CF-AMC's logbooks. While removing a tarpaulin, they accidentally pulled a flare tab and the Stearman burst into flames. The oil-splattered, unburned mail reached Detroit twenty-four hours later by train.

"For some time after, I was autographing oily letters which had been salvaged," laughed Burton.

Burton, described as "medium of height, thickset in his sheepskin-lined coat, keen-eyed and springy-stepped" by an eager *Mail & Empire* reporter, received a gold caterpillar pin with ruby eyes from the Irwin Air Chute Co., Inc. of Buffalo, N.Y. Burton was the first Canadian airmail pilot to save his life by parachute and the first Canadian to make a forced jump at night.

Canadian Airways did not hold Burton responsible and acknowledged that wireless could have prevented the accident. Without radio, London's ground staff was unable to contact him to advise that fog had closed down his destination at Detroit. The chief superintendent of Air Mail Service in Ottawa, G. S. Henning, pointed out in a telegram that Burton had "...put up a mighty good show on Saturday night and I think you have a lot to be thankful for that your guardian angel was hovering near."

Burton took a four-day break from his close call. While resting at home with Cile and their new son, Teddy, newspapers hounded him relentlessly. One journalist wrote that flying in "Cloudland" would remain a "trying and vexatious business" with disturbed schedules and choking fog banks. Nevertheless, he added, Burton's experience was accepted by aviators as merely "all in a day's work." The "iron-willed flier who looked unshaken and whose hands did not quiver after a sleepless night of adventure" must have agreed, for on December 23, he returned to duty.

Luckily, no more pilots were forced to bail out from Canadian Airways airplanes. Burton continued his frequent trips to Detroit at the time when the United States was embroiled in prohibition. In Canada, bootleggers could legally purchase liquor from Canadian distillers. As a result, a hangar at Windsor contained up to a half dozen American-registered airplanes in conditions that barely left them fit to fly. The owners valued their unairworthy wrecks only by what they could haul across the border.

"She's good for so many cases," said the rum runners, who preferred to be called "exporters." Every day, they telephoned a Detroit contact, cleared customs out of Canada and flew to unlighted fields under cover of darkness. It was risky business and placed the pilots under the obligation of the unsavory lawbreakers on both sides of the border. Several of Ed's acquaintances had "disappeared."

After landing in the United States, the pilots quickly swung into takeoff position with the engine running as burly gangsters unloaded. During one stopover at Windsor, Burton saw a large airplane with a massive section of missing wing fabric. Surprised by a party of police, the pilot had rammed the throttle forward, staggered airborne, hit a tree and limped across the river to Windsor. After hasty repairs, the same airplane went back to bootlegging the next night.

Burton hit the news again on March 31, 1932, when he encountered a seventy-eight mile-per-hour tailwind while flying Stearman CF-ASE from Detroit to Hamilton. After a late start from Wayne County Airport, his average 218 miles per hour over the ground resulted in a speed record of fifty-five minutes for the leg which normally took at least one hour and forty minutes. Newspapers also added hints of changes ahead for the hard-working mail pilots.

In the face of cutbacks necessitated by Canada's declining economic conditions, Canadian Airways pilots accepted pay cuts of 31 percent and watched federal experts pare away the lucrative airmail runs in spite of a 92.8 percent trip completion rate. Burton received word that the mail service would be discontinued on April 1, 1932, the day after his record-breaking flight from Detroit to Hamilton.

Some of his colleagues put their principles aside and went into flying booze and aliens across the border but few of these pilots survived. One friend was killed trying to master the art of flying an autogiro. The accident happened when he switched back to conventional control airplanes and misjudged his air-speed. Other friends simply drifted away from aviation.

Offered the opportunity of continuing with Canadian Airways at a reduced salary, Burton, with the support of Cile, who was every bit as adventuresome as Ed himself, declined. Preferring to seek new excitement elsewhere, he investigated rumors that an American organization was assembling a fleet of airplanes for a gold-hunting expedition into the Canadian north.

The World Glides By

Sitting up high in the heavens,
Control stick between my knees,
The engine roaring in front of us,
Plugging along through the breeze.
Limitless skies up above us
The world spread out under our feet
And away in the distance a purple haze
Where the earth and the heavens meet.
It seems as though we're not moving
We're suspended up in the skies
While the earth glides by beneath us
Ever changing before our eyes.
There are farmlands with cornfields and meadows
Hillsides covered with trees
Streams and lakes and rivers
Winding away to the seas.
And now from the distant horizon
Approaches a blanket of white,
As nearer and nearer it comes
And more distinct to the sight.
You can see it's the tops of the mountains
Covered o'er with a mantle of snow
The topmost peaks are lost in the mist
The deep silent valleys below.
Up there it's perpetual winter
As far as the eye can scan
A land of eternal snow and ice
Untrod by the foot of man.
They stand as they've stood for thousands
Nay, millions of years which have passed
They'll be there for millions of years to come
Rugged, majestic and vast.
They slope away down to the valleys
Where the silvery streams trickle through
Beyond are masses of forests
Then farmlands come into view.
The farms look like quilts of patchwork
Tiny patches of yellow and brown
The horses and cows in the fields look like ants

From our seat up above looking down.
The houses and barns all painted in white
Follow the roads in a line
Now the roads and fences run hither and yon
As if without thought or design.
But the roads lead off to the cities,
Here's a city now coming along
You can see twixt the chimneys and housetops
The crowds as they hustle and throng.
With the street cars and the motors
Which bustle in and out
While we look down and wonder
What it is all about.
But this is no time for dreaming,
For we must not be late
We've got a stack of mail on board
And the mail cannot wait.
Sitting up high in the heavens
Control stick between my knees
The engine roaring in front of us
Plugging along through the breeze.

CHAPTER FIVE

Mitchell Drinking Expedition to the Yukon

While Canadian Airways pilots were pioneering airmail routes in Canada, a trio of men, with backs bent and fingers numbed in glacial streams along the border of British Columbia and the Yukon, discovered yellow streaks in their gold pans. As the end of the warm weather season approached, shorter days forced them to scramble harder for as much of the precious metal as they could find.

Greed kept them in the mountains past the time when they should have trekked back to civilization. Cold, starvation and overwork soon killed two of the men. The survivor, who is remembered only as Hamilton, buried his partners as well as he could and gathered their hoard of gold. Nearly blinded by blizzards, he stumbled along snow-draped valleys and kept his precious moosehide poke tied around his neck. Staggering at last into the tiny community of Juneau, Alaska, he collapsed, weakened from scurvy and close to death.

Rumors drew mining promoter Thomas M. Mitchell to the dying Hamilton. He tried to bring him back to health but the hardships of the trail proved too much. Before the pain-racked prospector died in Mitchell's arms, he gasped out the approximate location of the find, or so Mitchell told anyone who would listen.

Mitchell, who had unsuccessfully prospected the area in 1929 and 1930, lost no time in traveling to Detroit to find backing for a large scale gold-seeking expedition. Although the cruel Depression had settled like a monstrous black cloud on a world of soup lines and idled factories, gold still held the power to excite men's imaginations. The idea of scooping fortunes from the ground seemed plausible, especially when emotions were stirred by stories written by the likes of Robert Service and Jack London.

Mitchell's tales of gravel creeks and potential bonanzas captured the attention of several affluent businessmen. On the alert for sensational stories, the *Detroit News* dispatched its corporate Lockheed Vega airplane across Canada in March, 1932, to an area close to the Liard placer district. Snow prevented detailed studies of prospective claims but the crew dug into the banks of the Finlayson River and reportedly found a few "colors."

Mitchell, described by author Dermot Cole as having an "...appearance of being rather shrewd," had silenced the skeptics. Within weeks, the Mitchell Exploration Co. Ltd. raised 150,000 dollars for an aerial assault on the gold fields. Backers claimed it would stem the Depression just as the Klondike discovery had helped the economy a few decades earlier.

Convinced the job would require a fleet of airplanes, former dental equipment manufacturer James H. Eastman became a partner. With Thomas Towle, he had designed the Eastman Flying Yacht which first flew in 1927. Sales brochures touted the wheelless flying boat as ideal for "...those who love the stinging spray of mile-a-minute speed across the water and the joyful indolence with rod and reel on the placid surface of a pine-rimmed lake."

In 1929, the Detroit Aircraft Corporation acquired the manufacturing rights and renamed the aircraft Sea Rover. Only sixteen were produced with a $10,000 price tag but five went to the Mitchell Expedition for the rock bottom price of $300 each. The organizers had no intention of using the "thoroughbreds" on Sunday jaunts to the untouched fishing grounds promoted by exuberant salesmen. Instead, they applied for and received Canadian registrations to enable them to work in the wilds of northern Canada.

While this was taking place in Detroit, Burton contacted friends who had mentioned the Mitchell Exploration Company. He saw in the venture an exciting, new opportunity since the future of Canada's airmail was much in doubt.

"Like most of the others, I agreed to go to work with them for little pay but for a stake in what we believed to be the certainty of huge profits," he said. "We were all mesmerized by the talk of panning gold in the mountains, hobnobbing with the likes of

Stampede John and Three-Fingered Ike of Klondike fame and visions of fame and fortune."

Burton's first look at the four-seat Eastman Sea Rover revealed what appeared to be a well-crafted airplane. The sleek machine with a flat-decked, boat-shaped aluminum hull had a maximum cruise range of 360 miles averaging ninety miles per hour at a fuel consumption of 10.56 US gallons per hour. Useful payload in the fore and aft cockpits totalled a meager 472 pounds after full fuel, oil and pilot.

"A very unlikely aircraft for freighting out in the bush where you had to load it down with extra gas in order to get back," said pilot Frank Barr, who joined the expedition in Alaska as a spare pilot. "You had your choice—carry freight and stay there or carry gas and get back."

The biggest drawback, the pilots noted, was the 185-hp Curtiss Challenger engine. In reality, it had been created by bolting two three-cylinder radial engines together and placing them on undersize steel mounts. One rumor circulated that the Challenger had been so unreliable, the U.S. Navy dumped an entire inventory into the ocean rather than release them to civilian markets.

"The Curtiss Challenger engine was rough, I mean rough," added Barr. "The pilot's line of vision was below the engine with the carburetor directly in front of his eyes. That engine gave me a lot of confidence. When I looked straight ahead, I thought I had two engines—at least I could see two carburetors."

At the time of the Mitchell Expedition, aviation was only twenty-nine years old. A transcontinental flight of five flying boats from Detroit into barely charted terrain almost untouched by bush pilots would be an incredible feat. Burton, hired partly because of his navigational expertise and Curtiss HS-2L experience, used maps scaled to fifty-miles per inch.

"Two hundred miles at a time were blank so we'd sketch in the major features and compare notes whenever we could," he said. "It also fell to me to help Jim Eastman keep the machines in the air as I was reasonably handy with a wrench."

Burton's letter to Lucille from the Hotel Fort Shelby in Detroit, dated Monday, May 23, 1932, outlined security measures that surrounded the expedition:

...Most of us were busy to-day buying odds and ends for the machine. My ship is to be CF-AST. Eastman flew it with me for a few minutes this morning to test it out. It is a dandy. We are to head for Sault Ste Marie first, then Port Arthur, then Winnipeg—then Edmonton. I will let you know the route from there as soon as I know.

They want us to keep it quiet where we are heading for as the Detroit News wants the story. I will subscribe for you. The news-photographer took photos of us to-day (sic) in groups and singly and our life history too...

...Apparently we are to go up the west coast, but they don't want us to say so to anyone as it may spoil our chances of staking....

On May 25, 1932, the expedition got underway. Burton, *Detroit News* pilot Frank Byerley and ex-RAF wing commander D. M. Emery joined Eastman and former U.S. Navy pilot J. J. "Red" Harrigan in a formation takeoff from the Detroit Yacht Club dock. Ten minutes later, they landed to clear customs at Windsor. Here, they made another dramatic departure and followed routes paralleling railroad lines and water bodies whenever possible. Each pilot planned to maintain his own Sea Rover and for safety's sake, all the airplanes stayed within sight of each other.

On Friday, May 27, 1932, Burton wrote to Lucille from Ignace, Ontario, where he was staying at the Young Men's Christian Association:

...I started with best intentions of writing a long descriptive letter each night but due to delays during the day with five machines which are all new and require adjusting, we have been making slow progress and arriving late each day. Then we have to tether the machines down safely for the night, fill

From a middle class English family, Edward C. Burton with his sister, Freda, never predicted that his future would one day carry him into the Canadian wilds.

Edward C. Burton expected to join the waves of Canadian airmen graduating from training schools in Canada and Texas.

Burton's first flight in a Curtiss JN-4 took place on October 13, 1917. Sent solo with minimum dual instruction compared to today's training standards, he soon became proficient in all aspects of military aviation.

This Curtiss JN-4, believed to be assigned to 45 Squadron of aerial fighting, was typical of Jennies which Burton flew. The OX-5 engine weighed at least 541 pounds and the fuel tank was supported by steel straps padded with tiny wood strips.

Taught to fly in "double quick time," it was not unusual for Curtiss Jenny pilots to come down in strange places. This one from 81 CRS damaged an engine maintenance shed.

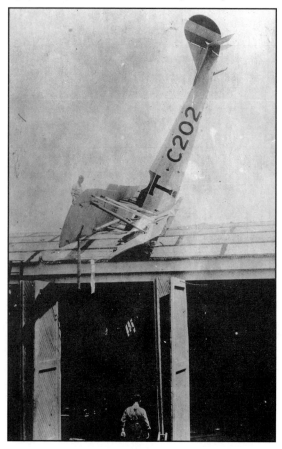

One pilot was seated in the rear cockpit of the lower Jenny when the other airplane landed on its tail. Neither pilot was injured.

During Burton's training in 1917, the need for Allied airmen became overwhelming. New Curtiss JN-4s, like this one, soon became masses of fatigued fabric, cracked wood and brittle tubing as student after student learned the elements of landings.

Jennies of 78 CTS at Camp Everman, Texas, became Burton's daily fare. It has been said that over 95 percent of Canadian and American pilots trained in World War I logged hours on the Curtiss. With engine, the first JN-4s averaged $8,160 each in 1917–18.

Edward C. Burton flew two Avro 504s in England after World War I ended. First flown in September, 1913, it had a wood girder-like fuselage. The pilot sat in the rear and cruise speed averaged 66 mph.

Built at Canadian Aeroplanes Ltd.'s plant at Dufferin and Dupont Street in Toronto, in August, 1917, Curtiss JN-4 C-282 was created of fabric from Trois-Riviere, Quebec, and ash from British Columbia's forests. Stationed at Leaside, it was eventually tested with one of Canada's first sets of airplane skis and later carried mail with Edward C. Burton at the controls.

For its day, Curtiss HS-2L G-CAOB was a large airplane. This example at Sioux Lookout in 1924 was out of commission for 35 days after striking a submerged rock on August 13. Curtiss G-CAOB was the first H-boat Burton flew.

While not able to find employment in Canada's aviation industry between 1919 and 1924, Burton spent much of his time in Northern Ontario timber camps. He happened on the scene just as the harsh bush country was becoming modernized with devices like this mechanical snow tractor.

In spite of summer heat, Burton (L) wore thick woolen clothing when flying the awkward H-boat. According to a note in Burton's papers, the first Liberty engine he experienced developed only 360-hp.

Refuelling H-boats was a complex operation. Several men were needed to balance a 45-gallon drum on a board across a pair of canoes. Gas caches were usually placed adjacent to railway lines.

The Saulteaux-Ojibway settlement of Pikangikum, northwest of Red Lake in 1924, was an occasional stop for Burton and his Ontario Provincial Air Service H-boat.

71

Curtiss HS-2Ls were notorious for mechanical failures. During the first year in service with 12 H-boats, OPAS pilots experienced 33 forced landings. Stripped gears, disconnected oil pipes, fouled plugs and defective carburetors accounted for many exciting stoppages.

Photo credit: Western Canada Aviation Museum

Buhl CA-5/Airsedan G-CATO built in 1928 by the Buhl Aircraft Craft Company at Marysville, Michigan, attracted Burton to National Air Transport. Formerly NC4356 in the United States, it was destroyed in a hangar fire at Toronto in 1935. Parked briefly during a southern Ontario barnstorming tour, its size attracted an abundance of joy riders.

Precautionary landings due to severe weather were commonplace on Montreal-Toronto mail runs. Maneuvering Fokker Super Universal G-CAWS into cattle fields surrounded by fences was not easy for Canadian Airways pilots like Burton (R).

Burton occasionally flew this Pitcairn PA-6 Super Mailwing for Canadian Airways. Built in 1928, it carried a smaller load than his regular Stearman and was damaged beyond repair in May, 1931.

It would have been a major undertaking for Canadian Airways ground staff to have taken this photograph at St. Hubert, Quebec, in 1931. All except one aircraft—Fairchild FC-2 G-CATU—have tailwheels. This and the following three photographs were originally one photograph, three inches high and two feet long.

Lucille Tervin and Edward Burton married in Florida on January 3, 1930. Lucille's first airplane ride had taken place in May, 1927, at Daytona Beach when she received a complimentary press ticket. After their marriage, she accompanied her husband whenever possible on mail runs and mercy missions into the Canadian bush country.

The inward bound *Empress of Britain* puts off air mail and takes on river pilots from the tug *Jolibert* at Father Point east of Rimouski, Quebec.

Pilots (L-R) Red Harrigan, Jim Eastman, Frank Byerley, William Emery and Burton at Juneau on June 10, 1932, did a remarkable job of flying their Sea Rovers across Canada and landing undamaged at Juneau.

The manufacturer claimed an 11 US gallon per hour fuel consumption at 85–90 miles per hour cruising speed with three people aboard the Sea Rover. It had a 36-foot wingspan—small compared to the Curtiss HS-2L's 74-ft, 1-in. squirrel cage wing.

After arrival at Juneau on June 10, 1932, pilots tied the Sea Rover fleet to a salt-water dock. Their arrival was heralded by the press and attracted sightseers from the community and outlying settlements. The piles enabled the dock to rise and fall with the tides.

Photo credit: British Columbia Aviation Museum

Trader Robert McCleary and his family at Teslin left a lasting impression on Burton. The Nisutlin Trading Post, named after a river flowing into Teslin Lake, became a gathering place for traders, trappers and pilots of British Columbia and the Yukon.

Right: During Burton's flights in northern British Columbia, Native totem poles still dominated many forest trails.

Below: Burton purchased his own gold pan at Juneau and tried his hand at washing gravel.

Burton, at far right wearing hat, enjoyed occasional outings with the expedition members on nonflying days. By the time this photo was taken, several families had joined the group in Atlin.

Some of the diggings for placer gold Burton encountered in British Columbia were complicated hand-built affairs requiring teams of men to operate.

Hazelton, on the Skeena River northwest of Terrace, was a stop Burton enjoyed, although he described the trip through the Rocky mountains as "...hard work going from place to place without conveniences for working."

Juneau was a bustling sea-going community which served as a staging area for gold seekers bound for Canada and Alaska in the 1930s.

A landing at Red Pass Junction, only five minutes flying time from Mount Robson, undoubtedly gave Burton, here with Sea Rover CF-AST, time to catch his breath before proceeding into the intimidating Rocky Mountain ranges.

When Amos Airways Curtiss Robin CF-AHE dropped from the Quebec skies on fur-buying expeditions, the Cree swarmed to the airplane. Trading came later and Fred Camelot's newly acquired furs would be packed into white cloth bags.

Native parents with children in tikanagans were typical loads for Amos Airways pilots. Warm and secure, the hand-made bark cradles were usually decorated lavishly with beads, quills and cloth strips.

Muskrat furs drying kept traders like Fred Camelot on the move. Usually the white tents were erected in the open so pilots Burton or Davis could locate them from the air.

Lazy John's wife and surviving family were removed from their squalid cabin. The harsh winter and surrounding spruce and bush forests provided little food sources for a woman and two children weakened by starvation.

GE Explorers Ltd. YKC-S Waco supported the gold prospectors in the Northwest Territories' Barrenlands. Burton frequently had little to tie the precious airplane to on rocky shorelines and spent many hours monitoring CF-AWH.

At Fort McMurray, Alberta, Burton took a few minutes to photograph CF-AWH while his passenger refuelled from 45-gallon gasoline drums.

The village belles at Pikangikum, north of Red Lake, Ontario, never wore full-length pants or anything resembling men's clothing during Burton's visits. Their heavy dresses and brown-ribbed socks were slight defence against seasonal mosquitoes.

Ontario Department of Lands and Forests officials encouraged Northern Ontario's trapping families to conserve beaver. Later, successful replanting revitalized the fur harvest.

Bushplanes were common at northern Ontario's native settlements but when Burton brought in provincial game officials with yellow Norseman CF-OBG, the entire community turned out. This meeting took place at Big Trout Lake, 239 miles northeast of Sioux Lookout. Most northern villages are now served by wheel-equipped aircraft.

Hudson's Bay Company posts often served as meeting places when Burton flew Ontario government officials to Northern Ontario Native reserves.

Beaver pelts were traditionally dried and stretched on willow frames in Northern Ontario Cree/Ojibway villages.

During the 1950s, tepees were common living and storage structures at Kasabonika Reserve, 242 miles northeast of Sioux Lookout.

Edward Cherry Burton at Orient Bay in the Vickers Vedette.

Prior to spring departure for Orient Bay, Burton prepares to air test Vickers Vedette G-CAND at Sault Ste. Marie. Mechanics are pushing the airplane into the St. Mary's River and will recover the wheeled dolly after it floats free.

Burton enjoyed the Vickers Vedette's spritely takeoff characteristics but later refused to fly it when age took a toll on the airframe and engine. Here at Sault Ste Marie headquarters, he prepares to depart for Orient Bay, accompanied by his family.

The Vickers Vedette made its first flight on November 4, 1924, from the St. Lawrence River at Montreal. Burton's favorite—G-CAND—was built in 1928 and removed from service in 1944. Former bush pilot Jake Siegel of Red Lake, Ontario, remembers it as being blown over a fence and destroyed in Sault Ste Marie in about 1944.

Transferring live "nuisance" beaver to areas where they prospered into a successful harvest of pelts was a duty Burton enjoyed with Noorduyn Norseman CF-OBO. Conservation officers F. W. MacKay (L) and George Wagner (R) on September 7, 1949, accompanied him on many such flights.

Ontario Department of Lands and Forests, Air Service Branch pilot Edward Cherry Burton shortly before retirement at Kenora, Ontario.

up with gas and oil and inspect them carefully—have a wash which is badly needed—find a place to stay at night—get a meal and finally go to bed....

...We stopped on an inland lake on the West side of Lake Huron for gas—a long lake with beautiful surrounding country and only about two houses in sight. Though the lake was about six miles long it had no name. After filling the tanks and having a cup of thermos coffee and sandwiches we took off again and headed for Sault Ste Marie. We passed over a couple of grain boats away off in the lake—almost out of sight of land—then over some beautiful islands—up to St. Mary's river and landed by the Ontario Provincial Air Service wharf at Sault Ste. Marie. We stayed over night at the hotel.

Thursday's flight was quite interesting—skirting around the North Shore of Lake Superior.

We landed twice on the way in the shelter of some beautiful islands—just an occasional freighter in the distance and finally the Sleeping Giant Island (a huge, natural formation visible from present-day Thunder Bay's shoreline) in the distance grew larger and larger till we arrived at Port Arthur Harbor and landed for the night....

In the air, the Sea Rovers handled well. However, extreme vibration from temperamental Challenger engines resulted in cracked mounts, leaking gas tanks, fouled plugs and broken oil lines. Everywhere they stopped, fishermen, trappers, railroad workers and others along the way offered help. Treated like royalty but reticent about divulging their exact destination, the pilots enjoyed the flight and knew they were making history.

After Windsor, they landed in an unnamed lake to refuel from gasoline kegs carried aboard and continued to Sault Ste Marie for an overnight stay. In the next few days, they crossed Northwestern Ontario, Manitoba, Saskatchewan and Alberta with the longest nonstop leg lasting two hours and fifty minutes.

"There has been considerable delay at some points on account of the machines and engines being new," Burton wrote to Lucille, who always showed interest in the piloting life of her husband. "To be sure of having them in sound condition, we go over them thoroughly. Now that they have had a fair amount of use, they are getting 'set' and will not require so much attention from now on."

Events soon proved his prediction wrong. After a three-day holdover near Edmonton because of poor weather and engine maintenance, the formation left South Cooking Lake on a Sunday afternoon. Forty miles west, a leaking gas tank forced Emery down on Wabamun Lake. The other aircraft also landed and waited until the line was resealed. Ready to go, Burton's CF-AST would not start and forced the group to stay the night.

At nine o'clock the next morning, watched by cheering crowds of Indians and a few whites standing along the railroad tracks, the fleet headed west. There was little wind and the airplanes accomplished faster groundspeeds than usual. By ten o'clock, farm land fell behind as scrub country, swamps, tiny pothole lakes and narrow rivers began dominating the foothill country.

While map reading, Burton noticed long white streaks spreading across the horizon. At first, they appeared to be banks of mist but he soon realized they were snow-capped mountains reflecting the sunlight. The Mitchell Expedition fliers had reached a milestone—their first flight into the Rocky Mountains.

Drawing closer, Burton distinguished needle sharp peaks high in a region of frost and crevasse-scarred rock walls. Leaving the rolling foothills, the fleet picked up the Athabasca River and slipped into a valley and along Brule Lake, the staccato of their cylinders reverberating from cliff to cliff.

The pilots simultaneously eased in their throttles and climbed to 8,000 feet. At that height, the Sea Rovers were higher than the snow line but still below peaks on both sides. Trees crowded the slopes and lower down, silvery streams bordered by bleached limbs and grasses hanging in sun-dried tufts wove into rapids and waterfalls. Occasionally, deep blue or green smooth-surfaced lakes caught the reflection of five minuscule airplanes passing overhead.

The formation followed the Athabasca River into clear air to Jasper and turned right to find the Fraser River. Five miles beyond the small trading and tourist community, pilot Red Harrigan turned back to a lake at the foot of a tremendous mountain. Burton joined him and discovered that Harrigan's Sea Rover had been consuming more fuel than the others. While they topped their tanks, a passing freight train reminded both men that the Great Depression had not been left behind.

"Riding inside boxcars or sitting on top of them were forlorn, ill-clad groups of men, all on the move and desperately hoping to find work," Burton said. "A plainclothes policeman with a pocket full of fifty cent pieces provided by the government patrolled the track and handed them to anyone who seemed more down and out than the others and sent him up to the station beanery for a meal."

Forty miles later, Burton and Harrigan found the three other Sea Rovers snubbed to the shore at Moose Lake. The party walked a half mile to a small hotel and returned after two hours. Off again, they passed through rain clouds along the twisting Fraser River and at one point, looked up at 12,972-foot Mount Robson. They dropped to 5,000 feet until the mountain ranges diminished into dense rolling forests.

Communicating by hand signals—no radios were light enough to carry in Sea Rovers in 1932—the group landed near Prince George two hours and thirty minutes after Moose Lake. The following day, they continued to Burns Lake and then Hazelton, where they hauled logs and boulders into place as tiedowns. An RCMP constable investigating the phenomenon of a flock of airplanes in his territory guided them to a hotel sided with wood slabs. The menu was moose.

"As was common in bush hotels in Northern Canada, if you wanted to eat, you sat at a large table with all other guests, no matter what their station," Burton said. "You ate without complaint whatever was put before you. It was usually pretty good."

Two more days put the Mitchell Expedition in Juneau, Alaska. Unfamiliar with tides and their effect on flying boats, the pilots tied the Sea Rovers in a neat row to an immense wharf. Ropes on the nose of each airplane prevented them from floating away while they checked into rooms at the Alaskan Hotel for one dollar a day. Almost immediately, Burton described the new sights to Lucille:

> ...This is a rum little town—about 4000—built largely on piles at the waters edge at the foot of the mountain. There are several nice stores here but no railway and only a short piece of road but a number of cars.
>
> One sees lots of tough looking men in heavy boots and quite a number of Indians. The boats come in two or three times a week. One boat came in late this afternoon so ECB will be off to the post office first thing in the morning....

Meanwhile, as the tide came in, the airplanes began nosing down into the seawater and were about to sink. A bystander rushed down to help before the pilots raced back. Before they could stop him, the man stepped from the wharf onto a Sea Rover's lower wing. His feet plunged through two layers of fabric and also damaged the wing tip float. Luckily, they retied the fleet without more damage.

After assisting in the repair of the hole with fresh fabric, glue and new wood, Burton returned to his room. Elated with the fact that the expedition had crossed Canada almost unscathed, he described the landscape to Lucille in one of his numerous letters: "With range after range of mountains high above coming down to a carpet of green timber and all reflected on the lakes as they passed by beneath us—lakes of brown, blue and even pink, fed by streams whose falls and cataracts of melted snow tumbled down from above," he wrote on June 11. "Before we of the Mitchell Expedition saw that country in the spring of 1932 probably not more than a few people had ever seen it."

After several days in Juneau, the group met more members from Detroit, including Tom Mitchell who had traveled by boat and train. While the prospectors purchased bed netting, fishing tackle, "Skeeter Dope" or whatever they needed to survive, the pilots busied themselves inspecting their Sea Rovers before the final leg into the goldfields.

Burton arranged for a welder to repair his Challenger's fatigued engine mounts. One evening, with the job barely completed, he dropped off to sleep only to be wakened at 1:30 A.M. by Mitchell.

Stories of the Mitchell Expedition had been front-page news for days and at least two other groups planned to move in on the rumored discovery. One, Mitchell exclaimed, was led by the famous "Stampede John" O. Stenbratten who was supposed to have participated in every goldrush in the north.

"We've got to get going," Mitchell implored. "Stampede John's hired his own airplane and plans to get there ahead of us."

Quickly slipping into his clothes, Burton rushed Mitchell to CF-AST where Detroit lawyer Wes Gallogly waited in the dim morning light. The possibility that Stampede John could cause havoc with the expedition's plans was a serious concern. The rules of the mining game clearly stated that the first person to stake and register a claim owned the ground.

"Have you got a gun, Ed?" Mitchell demanded.

"A gun? Sure, I always carry a .22 rifle for partridge in case of a forced landing," Burton replied. He did not mention that he had an aversion to revolvers since the incident in Harlan.

"Not that kind of gun; a revolver," Mitchell snapped. He pulled one from under his jacket and opened the action. "You should have brought one; there's likely to be shooting on the diggings."

Later, Burton watched Mitchell blow the head off a partridge from thirty-five feet away.

Burton, Mitchell and Gallogly climbed into CF-AST and left the water just as Juneau's street lights blinked off at 2:30 A.M. They flew south along Douglas Island and turned left toward the Taku River. After crossing the boundary along the Alaskan Panhandle into British Columbia, Burton reached a point where three valleys joined.

The river, bounded by spruce and cottonwood curling into the water, became a series of low gravel bars with the massive Taku Glacier dominating the north shore. On the right, sides soared as high as 8,250 feet and another glacier—the Wright— kept the valley in shadow.

Burton spotted several small log buildings, lumber piles, a cluster of ash-dotted tents and a wharf flanking a ramshackle warehouse. This was Tulsequah, an eight-hour boat ride or forty-minute Sea Rover hop, where Mitchell had prepositioned a gasoline cache of 5,000 gallons by steamboat. Touching down on the swift-running river dotted with floating, sullen tree trunks bobbing in frothy patches looked dangerous.

"By landing downstream, it was possible to manoeuvre fairly accurately and by swinging around quickly into the current, we were able to taxi up in the shelter of an island to the gas drums," Burton said. "It was an inhospitable resting place for our easily damaged machines so we lost no time in refueling and were on our way."

Burton climbed as high as he could, passing innumerable small rivers on both sides. Never an outstanding performer in a climb, the fully loaded Sea Rover gained height more easily when flown in the rising warm air on the sunny side of the valley. Once, the noisy Challenger startled a herd of mountain goats feeding beneath the snow line.

"One could see places where masses of rock had broken off the mountains and gone crashing down below, snapping off the huge firs and pines like matchsticks," Burton recalled. "The river became a torrent with very few places where an airplane could land. With the sun's heat absorbed by the dark trees and rocks, the mountaintops covered by cooling snow and the constantly shifting wind, the air became very rough."

At Atlin, a tourist and trapping community of 500, sixty miles east of Skagway, Alaska, they had breakfast, refueled and carried on to Carcross in the Yukon. At every stop, Mitchell and Gallogly discussed mining claims and arranged for supply caches. They continued to Whitehorse for the night and were questioned by RCMP constable F. R. Mason about the lack of a "declaration of export." Mason, however, allowed them to proceed.

"After leaving Whitehorse, we flew over the Whitehorse Rapids on the Lewes River where many old-time miners drowned on their way to the Klondike," said Burton. "The river takes a sharp bend between high rocky banks before it comes to the falls. The old timers rafting downstream with all their food and equipment couldn't see the falls 'til after they rounded the bend."

Burton refueled at Carcross, then flew back to Atlin. Next day, he returned to Tulsequah which served as a staging point for the first phase of the expedition. No one saw any sign of Stampede John—Mitchell had won the race.

As events turned out, Stenbratten, who died in Whitehorse during the mid-1970s, never caused a problem. Burton discovered the man was far from being the swashbuckler type portrayed by northern poets. The well-known character was actually a scruffy, smelly individual with few, if any, redeeming characteristics. His only positive attribute appeared to be an uncanny ability to handle a gold pan.

The excitement of exploring new country soon passed. Most of the pilots used their free moments to write home. The life was not a difficult one, as Burton said in a letter to Lucille:

June, 1932
Tulsequah, B.C.
...I am sitting on my bed as I write this. Two of us share a nice large tent with a stove to keep things comfy.
I picked up a touch of 'flu' at Juneau the other day and felt tough. There was another fellow in town from the camp and he wanted an aeroplane ride so I let him come back with Emery and I came back on the river boat which runs in for supplies. I still have a slight cold left but am feeling O.K. again now....
...Three of the remaining four of our planes flew down from Atlin this morning to take in some prospectors but the weather was not fit for them to return. To-night it is raining steadily, the clouds are low over the mountain tops and there are wisps of fog along the valley....
...I have received a check for my last months work and may open an account here for part of it and send the balance to you—depending on what banking facilities I can find.
I have been assured that there is lots for me to do and may take a turn in flying one of the other planes or may go in on a prospecting party. I don't expect to make a fortune this summer, but do not see why I cannot make something out of staking some claims.

Red Harrigan and Frank Byerley have been in to the 'diggings' and say that reports from there are very good. There is a considerable gamble in prospecting but I will draw the pay as usual and may be able to make a small 'stake'....

...I told you in a previous letter about our starting off early in the morning to get ahead of Stampede John.

He flew in with a fast plane as far as Carcross—going there direct. I had to land at Tulsequah and Atlin and arrived at Carcross just after the other plane arrived there, but we found that Stampede was to charter a plane which was at Atlin. Mitchell got over the difficulty by chartering the other plane to help fly our men in and give our other pilots a chance to fix up their engines after their flight from Detroit—at the same time holding up Stampede from going in to our diggings....

The pilots settled into the dangerous work of supplying prospectors dropped off at isolated lakes. Since the airplanes carried little fuel, they flew dozens of trips "spotting" or placing gasoline kegs at selected locations. Carefully marked on primitive, sometimes hand-sketched maps, these caches extended the Sea Rovers' range.

On June 20, the Mitchell Expedition pilots moved to Atlin. From this base, they routinely flew sixty-four miles northeast to Teslin, B.C. and another 140 miles northeast to Frances Lake in the Yukon. The possibilities of engine failure compelled the Sea Rovers to fly in pairs wherever they went.

Sometimes, when the day's work was finished, pilots tried gold panning on their own. On one occasion, Burton and Mitchell trudged up a valley to prospect at a place Mitchell said might have been the site of Hamilton's strike. He shoveled gravel into a pan and began showing Burton how to wash it with creek water. Almost immediately, a thin yellow line appeared on the inside rim. A seasoned prospector working nearby examined it carefully. One look was enough. He emptied the contents on the ground and spat in disgust.

"That there's gold leaf," he snarled. "That's come from heaven knows how far down the mountainside and been pounded out so thin there's no weight to it. Why, it'd take a bushel to make a wedding ring."

Looking back on the incident weeks later, Burton realized that the prospector's words had sounded the death knell for the expedition.

Burton's most troublesome duty consisted of maintaining the cantankerous Challengers. While inspecting the engine mounts of CF-AST, he discovered one cracked beyond repair. With limited access to the outside world and lack of facilities, no one knew how long it would take for a replacement part to arrive. The wait put a "serious cramp" on his flying activities. However, he used the downtime helping the other pilots.

Sometimes, Burton traveled to Juneau where he learned what he could from itinerant prospectors. The old hands told him that some companies bought claims for fabulous sums. So far, however, sizeable gold deposits had eluded every member of the Mitchell party. After the group had expended fortunes seeking the elusive metal, Seattle mining engineer Harry Townsend surveyed the prospects. He pointed out that the bonanza was not worth more than two cents a pan. It began to look as if the entire project had been a ruse dreamed up by Mitchell, who was now looked upon as being nothing more than a opportunistic "dream merchant."

Tension spread throughout the camps. Eastman considered the matter a personal affront since he had induced his Detroit friends to invest. Now, with hopes of a major strike fading, Eastman felt responsible. In fact, Juneau's *Daily Alaska Empire* began reporting that "stampede rumors all failed of confirmation." One story claimed that enough gold came out of a hole in a day to pay for an airplane. The growing number of men racing north had given credence to a possible Klondike-style gold rush and encouraged nearly thirty gullible investors to buy stock.

Not long after the expedition members discovered that the so-called big strike was mere gold leaf, they decided Mitchell had to be removed. On July 24, they asked Burton to fly him out to Teslin on the pretext he was being taken to examine some diggings in several nearby valleys. After mooring to a buoy, Burton, a helper and Mitchell began rowing toward shore to leave Mitchell at a lodge.

When the wily promoter discovered the deception, he became furious to the "verge of temporary insanity" and refused to get out of the boat. Burton flew the seething promoter to Atlin where they encountered Jim Eastman and some of the members of the party on the beach.

Burdened with Mitchell again, Eastman decided that the only way to be rid of the schemer was to pick a fight. He called Mitchell a "miserable son-of-a-bitch" and the battle began. They kicked, gouged, grappled and punched until pulled apart. The score included a "pippin" black eye and serious bruises for Mitchell. In Eastman's case, his thumb had been chewed so badly, it was nearly severed. Both men were attended to at Atlin's small clinic.

At the clinic, a doctor implored Burton to keep Eastman quiet. In a tiny room, Burton found his friend reclining with a heavily bandaged arm in a sling. Recovering from the anaesthetic, Eastman's mind was not yet clear.

"How's Mitchell?" Eastman asked. Burton replied that Eastman had done an excellent job. His opponent was "all banged up."

"Hot dog! Hot dog! Hot dog!" Eastman yelled, his arms swinging as if he were reliving the battle. To Burton's consternation, the sling and surgical dressings flew off.

Stockholders officially declared the Mitchell Exploration Company closed on July 5 and Mitchell, at the polite but persuasive urging of the RCMP, went south via Skagway the next day. The remaining personnel, reorganized under the leadership of Wes Gallogly and Eastman, decided to carry on their search for gold. Burton continued moving gasoline and freight with CF-ASW but now, the disheartened group held little hope of discovering worthwhile claims for later sale to mining firms.

During an evening's rest at one of the camps, mosquitoes and blackflies forced him to build a small smudge fire. While sitting in the smoke, meditating with pipe and sketch pad, he remarked on an immense, cube-shaped block of ice at the edge of the main glacier. It looked precarious and ready to fall any moment. Noticing Burton's interest, a prospector joined him.

"It's over twenty years since I came here," the old man said. "And I remember when I first saw that thing. I'd sit here and wonder when it was coming down, so you might have to stay around for a while yet."

Burton often flew into Teslin for supplies. In 1932, the trading post's population varied when winter drew the locals away for trapping. In the warm season, 150 people lived there including ex-RCMP corporal R. McCleary, his wife and two children, who ran the Nisutlin Trading Post. Two other white men managed a small store and a lone RCMP officer upheld the law. Scattered packs of semiwild husky dogs joined the welcoming committee whenever a Sea Rover landed.

During one stop, several trappers told Burton what true northerners considered a winter shopping trip. McCleary's wife, described to Lucille in Ed's frequent letters as "not coarse looking at all but as tough as the country in which she lived," often took her two young daughters on a seventy-five mile dog team ride to Atlin.

With blankets, food, ax and rifle, she strapped on a pair of snowshoes and settled the girls into a sleigh. The first night, she made camp and after the next twenty-five miles, stopped again. Much of the journey involved tiresome trudging across windswept lakes and deep snow in sub-zero temperatures.

"On the third day, she would reach Atlin, do her shopping, visit friends and come back on the same trail," said Burton. "Although she was athletic, Mrs. McCleary was by no means rough. In fact, she'd walked to Atlin three weeks before one of her girls was born."

Burton kept busy in CF-ASW while waiting for Eastman's thumb to heal and for Sea Rover CF-AST's parts to arrive. In July, bad weather prevented reaching a party at Wolf Lake, forty-two miles northwest of present day Mile 790 on the Alaska Highway. Fearing the crew would starve, Burton followed the Morley River to Morris Lake into flatland surrounding the camp where he expected to find a sullen, hungry group. Burton was surprised that everyone was in high spirits. Eager to gossip, they invited him for supper.

"Have you anything left to cook?" he asked.

"We're not short. You can have your choice of moose, goose, fish or ptarmigan," answered a prospector.

The cook—a former real estate salesman named McKinney—not only prepared the fabulous meal, but had provided it. The previous night, he had hidden in a brush-covered area to wait for a moose. After an hour, he shot a large creature which dropped, but seconds later the antlered giant stood up. McKinney fired again. When he crept over to make sure the moose was dead, he discovered two downed animals instead of one.

Moving two tons of slippery meat to camp presented almost insurmountable difficulties, but the prospectors discovered a cached moosehide boat. Built by nomadic Indian people, the ribs and frame had been hewn by ax and tied with thongs. All stitching was sinew, and tree gum sealed the seams. No screws, nails or wire had been used.

By the first week of August, the pilots and prospectors knew for certain the venture was a farce and no one would be scooping buckets of gold from the creeksides. Almost all the "Argonauts," as a Juneau newspaper described them, abandoned the treasure hunt and were flown to Juneau.

MOOSE.

At Frances Lake, eighty-three miles north of Watson Lake, one final tussle took place when Byerley, under Eastman's orders, loaded the camp's flour sacks, sugar, oatmeal, rice and other foodstuffs for Tulsequah. Three prospectors had wanted to stay behind and needed the supplies to carry them over until next spring. Instead of grubstaking the trio, Eastman insisted on returning the food to a trading post for credit.

"Out of sympathy for the underdog and my resentment at such stupidity, I removed the distributor rotor from ASY," said pilot Frank Barr who took over Harrigan's flying duties when he was called back to the United States. "Eastman bowled me over and started going through my pockets. It was no contest. He was a little taller, nearly twice my weight and with the help of the other pilots, the outcome was certain."

One member of the party drew a revolver but no shooting occurred when the missing rotor reappeared from Barr's pocket. On this sour note, the needy prospectors were denied enough provisions to sustain them over the winter and a series of flights between Atlin, Teslin and Tulsequah began. By the time the last Sea Rover grounded to a halt, no trace of the Mitchell Expedition remained.

Within days, the pilots, except for Barr who established his own air charter service in Alaska, left the north. Eastman later returned to form a successful mineral exploration company. One man ruefully described the summer's activities as the "Mitchell drinking expedition" because "...precious little gold was found but a lot of whisky found its way down the hatch."

Burton wrote a sad report to Lucille shortly thereafter:

...This venture did not turn out as well as anticipated for I was not able to stake anything worth while so did not stake a claim at all. The country has wonderful possibilities but this show has been so badly handled. I think I shall be able to get my salary till the end of August and expenses home without any difficulty, but our finances will probably have gone behind a bit....

...Yesterday evening I took the last man down to Tulsequah (three of us went together—each with a passenger and camp equipment) and returned last night just before dark.
It is a great relief to have them all back again safely. This afternoon a number of us drove up the creek together to see some of the mines and study their methods. I took my gold pan along and panned about fifty cents worth of gold which I hope to bring proudly home.
We now have to dispose of the five aeroplanes. I am trying to make a deal for one, hoping to fly it at least as far as Vancouver and make something on it if possible....

On August 8, the organizers began offering the Sea Rovers for sale. Some sold for commercial use and the last working one flew on September 3, 1945, with the Columbia Development Company in Atlin until converted to a boat. Accidents accounted for at least two and several went into storage. In later years, enthusiastic volunteers of Victoria's British Columbia Aviation Museum restored CF-ASY to original condition and placed the silver-hulled aircraft on permanent public display.

As for the infamous Mitchell, he was last seen in 1934 at Dease Lake, B.C., 152 miles southeast of Atlin, where he claimed another rich find. He and his comrades built several cabins and lived in them for two years before an American backer investigated the diggings. Mitchell quickly left Canada before the man arrived.

Burton considered buying one of the Sea Rovers to establish a charter business in Ontario. With little money to show for the season, he dropped the idea and boarded the CN steamship SS *Prince Rupert*. On August 15, 1932, a wire to Lucille announced his arrival in Vancouver. After a brief unsuccessful job search and a visit with his friend, Carter Guest, he boarded an eastbound train and ended forever his association with Eastman Sea Rovers.

In later years, Burton admitted to having been taken like a country rube but accepted his loss and moved on.

CHAPTER SIX

Fur Freighting
and Husky Hauling in Quebec

In Toronto, Burton discovered that employment situations for pilots, regardless of experience, had improved little. The government now issued few airmail contracts to Canadian air services or airlines and, although flying clubs survived, not many prospered. Desperate for some means to remain in aviation, Burton was relieved to find at least one job offer come his way from Minneapolis, Minnesota, on September 8, 1932.

An American group had decided to sponsor a trans-Atlantic crossing with a twin-engine amphibian called a Sikorsky S-38. Owned by a millionaire, the huge airplane carried enough fuel for 1,100 miles and had a wing span of over seventy-one feet. The route, starting from Lake Minnetonka near Minneapolis, included stops in Toronto, Montreal, Halifax and St. John's before flying to Europe via Greenland and Iceland. A tour of the continent would follow.

"Under my command with you as chief pilot and no departure will be made against unfavorable weather reports," telegrammed promoter P. T. McCarty. "Financial arrangements straight salary and expenses paid percentage of net profits accruing to flight as bonus Stop Particularly anxious to know your experience with boats and north country."

Burton investigated the proposal and found that the crossing had been poorly planned. No provisions for fuel were considered. He also discovered that the Sikorsky, which supposedly cruised at 129.5 miles per hour, would be carrying five passengers and three crewmen. Challenging as an ocean hop may have appeared, Burton judged the undertaking to be foolhardy and decided to decline.

To support Lucille and Teddy, he labored in the Toronto offices of Watts & Watts Brokers far from his recent world of turquoise lakes and mountain backdrops. Finally, he and Lucille invested their savings in renting Avro Avian CF-CDT at the London Flying Club to renew his instructor's rating.

At the end of flight testing at Camp Borden on September 17, 1934, Burton's first flight instructing job was at the Windsor Flying Club which offered 40-hp Taylor E-2 Cub CF-ARA to its members. During refresher training, he occasionally rented the Cub himself to take his wife and son aloft. Edward C. Burton, Jr. went for his first airplane ride on October 25. "Very interested" was the logbook comment, but it was not until after his father's death years later that the junior Burton learned to fly.

Burton moved on to the Ottawa Flying Club where he carried sightseers over the capital's copper-topped parliament buildings. Most flights took place in an Avro 594 Avian, a two-seat biplane which cruised at eighty-seven miles per hour and weighed 1,435 pounds fully loaded.

Besides providing a pay check, the Ottawa Flying Club had the bonus of being an unofficial gathering place for bush pilots from Ontario and Quebec. Burton picked up a tip that Dominion Skyways of Rouyn needed a pilot. Before long, an Ottawa newspaper reported that "the popular instructor at the Ottawa Flying Club" had accepted a new position.

"Dominion Skyways didn't waste much time and sent me to St. Hubert to pick up Fairchild FC-2W2 CF-AHG," said Burton. "I took it to Rockcliffe where they did a changeover from wheels to skis and then, I headed out to Rouyn where Peter Troupe ran the company's Fairchilds and Wacos."

Cabinfuls of canvas tents, dust-covered miners and empty fuel drums did not bother Burton but he quickly became discouraged with Dominion Skyways' dictatorial attitudes. While keeping his eye open for other avenues of work, he encountered former Deseronto pilot William J. Davis. An ex-Jenny instructor, Davis had acquired two bushplanes and intended to open a flying service in competition with Dominion Skyways. He needed another pilot and accepted Burton for his headquarters in Amos.

The move was an easy one for the Burton family since Amos was only forty-eight miles northeast of Rouyn. The French-speaking community's position at the junction of the

Transcontinental Railway and Harricana River made Davis' base ideal for the mining industry and moose-hunting Cree bands in the nearby forests, waterways and the vast Canadian Shield.

The Indians who harvested fur-bearing creatures traditionally sold their catches after long journeys by canoe or dogsled to Hudson's Bay Company posts. To circumvent this, some non-Native entrepreneurs chartered airplanes to intercept trappers at their camps. Burton enjoyed these assignments since he experienced first hand the lifestyles of nomadic Cree relatively unaffected by the white man's ways.

Many Native families camped close to Amos during the open water season and slipped away before the cold weather arrived. Most depended on canoe travel along the Harricana River. Burton marveled at the expertise required in maneuvering overloaded vessels packed to the gunwales with blankets, cooking pots, tents and traps. Giggling children and snarling dogs served as ballast and women wrapped in blankets with their infants rode astride the cargo. One man commanded the stern and another watched from the bow. Each swung a heavy, hand-carved paddle.

"When the canoe came near the swift water, the men paddled like fury to gain the speed they needed for control," Burton said. "Then, just as they hit the swirling rapids, the bowman sprang to his feet and stood right up with one foot on each gunwale, looking for rocks ahead, dipping his paddle first on one side, then the other, to swing the canoe."

The stern man watched his partner closely and added his strength. In a superb display of teamwork, they manipulated their way safely through swift, debris-dotted white water made more

dangerous by ugly spears of broken branches, until they reached calmer pools beyond the rapids. Burton never saw a canoe capsize.

Burton logged dozens of hours in Davis' 1928 225-hp Fairchild FC-2. Registered G-CANB, the fabric-covered, wood-winged freighter could fly over 500 miles at ninety-five miles per hour. The average Amos Airways payload with full fuel totalled slightly more than 700 pounds. The Fairchild gave little trouble, although in one case Burton lost a rear float cover while carrying a load of volatile dynamite and barely made it to Senneterre before dark. He pumped out the compartment, repaired the hole and spent the night in what bush pilots referred to as the "Fairchild Hotel."

An aggressive fur buyer named Frederick Camelot became a regular Amos Airways customer who often hired Burton to fly him to remote camps. Personal service counted for a great deal and the former airmail pilot's reputation for getting along with customers quickly spread—a necessity since trips often lasted for days. Luckily, Lucille, who had arrived with Teddy in Amos on July 29 after a fifty-minute flight from Rouyn, was a resourceful woman and supported her husband's absences.

The Fairchild always carried a full load of trade goods. Sometimes, fur buying took place while Burton idled the engine to prevent the oil from thickening. When he returned to Amos, the merchandise would be gone and replaced by stacks of tightly packed hides.

Most bargaining went on in cabins or skin tents. Indians from adjoining camps entered the largest dwelling and sprawled on benches or leaned against the walls. Camelot would shake hands with each band member and use the Native greeting *kway-kway, kway-kway*. After formalities, the elders invited Camelot and Burton to sit.

"Camelot would crack jokes with the men and talk about everything except furs. Sometimes, somebody'd draw out a lustrous beaver or lynx skin from a packsack and hand it to him," said Burton. "He'd look it over casually and hand it back as if furs were the last things in the world that interested him. While all this went on, the Fairchild's engine would be getting cold or if I'd left it running, it'd be using gas."

Next, Camelot produced a treat, usually a bag of oranges, and handed them around. In one instance, an old crone with a kerchief covering her long, gray-streaked hair hesitated. She had never seen fruit from Florida.

"Come, have orange," Camelot urged. "Make you have baby."

She took the fruit and everyone laughed. Before long, only one orange remained. Camelot offered it to Burton.

"No thanks, you eat," Burton said. "I don't want a baby."

Finally, they began discussing prices. Children with tiny weasels received fifty cents per pelt. Each fur went into a large sack Camelot placed behind him. Every transaction led to a note in a tattered account book as payment for supplies provided on credit weeks before.

The Cree were skilled negotiators, as Burton learned. One elder in a raspy whining tone lamented his lack of success as a trapper. He added, using a stuttering mixture of Cree and English, that recent journeys upstream netted him nothing. His arms flailed to show the direction he took and the hardships endured. No furs, no furs, he whimpered again, then paused.

"But my wife, she got fur when me away. She do go way down river by herself and catch good fox," he said.

Camelot bought the fur and explained later that the old man likely caught the creature himself but wanted cash. Owing Camelot several grubstakes, anything he earned would be held back on account. However, the trapper's wife had to be paid directly. The man kept the best part of his furs until spring know-

107

ing they would be worth more. Worse, Camelot knew, the old trapper would probably seek a rival buyer to whom he was not indebted and thus, could collect cash for his pelts.

Once, a Cree trapper named Thomas Rankin chartered Amos Airways to drop him, his family and two large husky dogs at Wawagosik Lake in late December. One of the semiwild animals slipped from his collar during the flight in the Fairchild and attacked his sleigh mate before Rankin could restore order. After landing and unloading, Burton returned to Amos and except for a logbook notation, he forgot about the trip until another, days later.

Touching down on a snow-covered lake forty miles from where he had originally left Rankin, he kept the engine idling while Camelot conversed with several trappers. Burton saw one of the group break away and approach the airplane. To his surprise, it was Rankin. Without map or compass, the man had crossed miles of rolling country covered in thick forest growth.

"Don't need no map," explained Rankin. "Me, I hunt and trap here all my life in this country with my father and remember my way. Don't need no compass around here. Look, you, all trees slope east."

Burton had never noticed the peculiar slant of northern trees. Shutting off the Fairchild's engine, he walked across the ice to see for himself. Sure enough, Rankin was right; the trees did have a distinct lean to the east. Bush dwellers always knew which way trees slanted in their part of the world and used the knowledge to find their way from camp to camp.

While Camelot bagged his furs, Burton took the opportunity to learn more Indian lore. He remarked to Rankin that he rarely saw sickness in the closely packed tents and tepees in which forest people lived. Sniffling, runny-nose colds were uncommon.

"Do Indians use herbs for medicine?" he asked.

"Yes, use wild cherry. White man like wild cherry now, too," Rankin replied. "Mostly we use cedar bark. Tea made from cedar bark very good. Cedar poultice very good too. If have appendix pain, I put on cedar poultice and I think get better."

Natural remedies did not always work. Burton discovered this sad fact during a flight with a doctor to Splendid Island, a small settlement on the Harricana River where a flu epidemic raged. For weeks, seventeen band members, including a 100-year-old woman, lay in head-splitting agony with body temperatures of over 100 degrees Fahrenheit. In this case, the white man's pills took effect almost instantly. On the way home, the doctor explained that northern Natives usually responded well to modern medication since they rarely used any.

Medical problems were not the only things that intrigued Burton, whose curious mind constantly compelled him to investigate anything out of the ordinary. In the course of his work, he frequently encountered startling examples of severe hardship and courage. On a flight to the Allard River, eighty-one miles north of Amos, he landed at a cabin on the river bank. No one seemed to be home. As the Fairchild's engine noise faded into the surrounding conifers, a young woman and a huge one-armed individual on snowshoes rounded a bend in the river.

Back at Amos, Camelot explained that the trapper had mangled his arm in a bear trap and, fortunately, friends happened by. They amputated the shattered member with an ax and hunting knife, and then plunged the dripping stump into a pail of hot lard to stop the bleeding. In spite of the lack of anesthesia, the grim procedure proved successful. The man survived and continued trapping with his daughter, described by another pilot as "two ax handles broad." By northern standards, the pair were successful in wresting a living from the wilderness.

On a December morning, an RCMP officer contacted Amos Airways for an airplane to Lemoine Lake, fifty miles north. There, a starving family had been reported.

Burton had just completed a trip in the Fairchild and required fuel. Rather than wait, he switched to a small 1924 model Curtiss C-1 Robin registered CF-AHE. Powered by a Challenger engine, it carried less payload than most bushplanes. Nevertheless, the pilot and two RCMP passengers soon found themselves cruising north above the spruce tops.

Thirty minutes later, they landed at Lemoine Lake after spotting a tiny cabin a short distance in from the shoreline. Like most Cree dwellings, it was placed far enough into the trees that winter winds rarely reached the flimsy structure. The camp belonged to Lazy John, a man of monstrous size whose bulk made traveling in the thickly forested countryside difficult. Not really lazy, his plodding ways left the impression he barely moved, but the nickname stuck.

Usually when an airplane dropped in from the Quebec sky, cabin dwellers scrambled outside to see the "big white bird." This time, however, no one came out as the policemen fastened their snowshoes and disappeared from sight pulling a small toboggan. Burton settled into the Robin to wait and shortly, the RCMP returned with two children.

"One was a pale, pinch-faced little girl around ten; the other, a boy about eight," Burton said. "Lazy John was out on his trapline somewhere but the mother followed behind in the path made by the toboggan. She carried a baby in her arms and another hatless, wide-eyed little boy clung to her skirt."

The woman wiped her eyes with a sooty, checkered apron as the officers lifted one of the boys and the girl into the airplane. Weakened and in worse shape than the others, they would be rushed to a hospital in Amos.

Before climbing back into their seats, the RCMP left several sacks of food for the mother and the remaining children. Burton eased in the throttle, and felt the mother watching as he turned to a heading for home. She never saw her daughter again. The next day, the child died from starvation in spite of the hospital staff's heroic efforts to save her.

Sadly, the suffering at Lemoine Lake did not end with the little girl's death. On a fur-buying trip three months later with Camelot in the Curtiss Robin, they circled the same cabin. Again, a lack of smoke from the chimney indicated trouble. Snowfall had long ago obliterated the ski tracks from the December landing. Watching carefully for slush holes, ridges and ruts, Burton landed to investigate.

Camelot stepped into the snow, dragged out his snowshoes and slipped then on. Minutes later, he pushed along the trail toward Lazy John's cabin. As Burton waited with the propeller slowly turning over, Camelot rushed back out of the bush.

"Ed, Lazy John's home this time but I don't know whether he's alive or dead. He didn't move when I talked to him,"

Camelot blurted out, exhausted from his run. "The woman and two kiddies are starving and they haven't got a crumb to eat and there's no fire."

"Why didn't you feel his pulse?" Burton asked. "That'd soon tell you if he's dead."

"Geez, I wouldn't do that," Camelot recoiled in horror. "He might be dead."

Burton shut down the engine, opened the emergency ration kit, selected an armload of cans of food and stuffed as many as he could into his pockets. With ax in hand and Camelot following, he ploughed his way to the cabin.

A typical trapper's shack, the structure was a twelve-foot square box thrown together from spruce and jackpine logs. A low opening covered by a strip of shredded canvas forced Burton and Camelot to stoop to their knees before entering. Frost covered the only window and light filtering through the cracked glass delayed their eyes from adjusting to the shadowed room. A pin-holed, rust-dappled stove stood in a corner.

On the earthen floor, the mother and her baby huddled together under a shawl. The boy, whom Burton had seen before, crouched beside her. A foot away on a bunk bed was big Lazy John with both eyes partially open. The remnants of a grease-spotted Hudson's Bay blanket covered the rest of his body.

The woman pointed first at Lazy John, then at the bloated stomach under the blanket to indicate her man was sick and could not provide. Her arms circled ten times to tell her visitors how many days the sun had gone around since Lazy John fell ill.

Burton pulled back the blanket to check Lazy John's pulse.

Lazy John was not just dead; his frozen, lifeless body resembled a gigantic slab of misshapen ice.

Burton and Camelot knew they could not leave Lazy John's family to fend for themselves this time. However, the Curtiss Robin lacked enough cabin space to take them to Amos. After a brief discussion, they slid the rock hard corpse outside and built a fire inside the ice cold cabin. They forced wood into the decrepit tin stove and heated food which the woman and her son gobbled ravenously. Now stronger, she fed the baby with particles she herself had chewed and inserted into its mouth with her fingers.

Next day, Lucille filled a packsack with sandwiches and a bottle of milk for the baby. At the cabin, the surviving members of Lazy John's family ate Lucille's food but were still too weak to walk to the airplane. Aided by an Amos Airways mechanic, Burton moved them by toboggan to the larger Fairchild Burton had selected for the flight. Lazy John stayed behind.

At Amos, the nursing staff placed the family in the same room in which the little girl had died months before. Knowing that winter frost would preserve Lazy John, Burton did not feel rushed to return to Lemoine Lake. A week later, he flew in an RCMP constable to bring out the body for burial.

Sometimes, hospital visits turned out to be educational experiences for the young Cree who lived their lives in sheltered bush country. Davis returned to base with a male youth scheduled for minor surgery. Accustomed to seeing mechanical miracles like Fairchilds or Curtiss Robins, he showed no fear of flying. Never having been away from his father's trap line, however, he received the fright of his life when the airplane landed at Amos and taxied to the parking area.

In the not surprising absence of motorized taxicabs, Amos Airways depended on a team of Belgian horses and a passenger sleigh. When the two massive, snorting creatures with long hairy tails stopped close to the Robin, the boy's terror knew no bounds and he nearly escaped before a hospital escort tackled him. It took nearly an hour to calm him down with a succession of ice-cream cones before Bill Davis convinced him the horses were not a pair of demented moose.

Each spring breakup, Davis and Burton taxied their airplanes from the ice and changed over to seaplane floats. Occasionally, Camelot demanded trips immediately after breakup when he had reason to be concerned about trappers who did not return to Amos. In one season alone, he extended their credit for a railroad boxcar load of flour. In desperation, he had to fly north to buy furs or face total bankruptcy.

On one trip, Camelot brought along a portable gramophone and several records. As Burton eased the Fairchild into the air,

Camelot watched for Indian canoes en route to Amos. The water ran dark with large trees overhanging the washed-out river banks. An emergency landing in the fast water and school-like clusters of detached tree stumps would be hazardous.

Banking sharply to his side, Burton noticed movement ahead and below the nose. Three large canoes, bottom side up in the process of being portaged past a channel of white-water rapids, looked like a long red caterpillar. Tiny figures with packs on their backs followed. Behind them, several dogs spread out in a thin dotted line. He pointed down, drawing Camelot's attention to the tableau below.

"Damn, we missed them," moaned Camelot, as he stared at the faces looking up at the circling seaplane. The rapids prevented a landing but soon, two more camps appeared. A low pass revealed that only one person remained, a figure which looked like an elderly woman.

Further north, the river broadened and the current slowed as the dense forests thinned into stunted trees. A wisp of smoke wafted snakelike, almost straight up from a smoldering camp fire. Suddenly, sunlight flashed off a canoe pulled up on shore. Burton landed but to Camelot's dismay, they discovered that the Indian family had stopped only to boil a pot of tea. A competitor had already bought their furs.

Hours later and after several more disappointing landings beside furless families, approaching darkness forced an overnight stay beside a small island. Nearby, two huge Rupert's House freighter canoes and bluish camp smoke indicated another Native group settled in on a sand beach.

"In spite of the daylight left, Camelot didn't go near the Indians to trade furs. We tied the Fairchild to a couple of trees and secured the controls then sat back near our campfire, cooking bacon and eggs," Burton said. "All of a sudden, Camelot reached into his pack and brought out the gramophone. He cranked the thing up and put on a record."

With music floating on the evening breeze, it wasn't long before darkened faces under wool caps and calico kerchiefs peered through the bushes. As the crowd gathered, Camelot shook their hands and greeted each of them with *"kway-kway."*

After several records wound down, the men paddled back to their camp and returned with bulging bags of beaver, fisher, lynx, martin, mink and muskrat. The wily buyer examined each one, selected the best and placed them in his canvas storage bag. Camelot then opened a package of candies and distributed them to the children. When the darkness made trading difficult, the Indians left for their own tents.

As Burton and Camelot were breaking camp in the morning, two men who had visited the previous night paddled to the Fairchild. Each one lifted out a bag of furs.

"Found these," one said. "Didn't know we had them."

With the new furs added to his collection, Camelot later explained that the cunning trappers had known about the bags. This was the Indian way of having the last word. Returning to Amos, the Fairchild's seatless freight compartment bulged with pelts. In the warmth of the airplane, fat from every type of northern animal melted into the upholstery and permeated their clothes but Fred Camelot was saved from bankruptcy.

Veteran pilots routinely developed their own estimates as to what weather might have in store. Often they left their bases knowing they might be forced to land quickly and wait for clear skies. Burton kept a graph of daily conditions tacked to the wall of the Amos Airways office. His meticulous record keeping helped him spend less time away from home than most of his contemporaries. Nevertheless, late passengers or unpredictable storms could catch even the most experienced northern pilots by surprise.

Sometimes, pilots removed their sleeping bags and extra survival rations to make room for more cargo on short trips. On a run in the Fairchild hopping back and forth between two little lakes, Burton took off with nothing more than an engine tent beneath his freight. While returning to Amos, a fast-moving blizzard crossed his path. He pushed on, hoping to find a trading post or cabin for temporary shelter. As visibility lessened and lowering ceilings forced him closer to the ground, he barely missed striking treetops before finding a landable lake. Once down, he taxied the skiplane to shore, donned his snowshoes and plodded into the shelter of a few overhanging spruce trees.

Fighting through thigh-deep snow and barely able to see, he dragged the engine tent into the trees and erected it between a pair of tree trunks as shelter from the cold wind. He built a fire and settled in as the snow changed to sleet. When the fire burned down, the cold woke Burton and forced him out into the snow to grope for more firewood. He had kept his ax inside his parka, knowing he would perish if he lost it in the night. The sound of a pack of wolves howling nearby did nothing to contribute to his comfort.

"Funny thing, you know, it doesn't matter how often you're told that wolves never attack healthy human beings," he remarked later. "When you hear them in the dark, you move a little closer to the fire and grip your ax a little tighter."

Expecting to leave at daybreak, Burton was disappointed to find the wind increasing to gale force. To pass time and prepare for an eventual departure, he struggled from the relative comfort of the canvas and cleared the Fairchild's wings of wet snow. His only nourishment consisted of a single pack of stale Bovril, a powdered beef extract accidentally left in the airplane when he removed its ration kit.

Temperatures plunged to -30°F and caused the lake ice to crack and boom day and night. Burton slept at intervals sipping the hot liquid and keeping the ax handy as wolves howled from invisible hills.

Lucille believed her husband was resting comfortably in a wilderness trading post or some nearby settlement. Untroubled, she went about the business of caring for Teddy and looking after their tiny, rented bungalow. Three days after Burton's departure, she heard a skiplane pass overhead.

Shortly, Ed staggered in, face blackened from his camp fire and clothes sooty and singed. Long, unlaced boot laces nearly tripped him as he dragged his ice-caked boots across the floor. Lucille began preparing the only hot beverage that came to hand—Bovril. He drank it anyway because he loved her and never complained, but he could never bring himself to drink Bovril again.

Lucille and Teddy went to Florida to escape the frozen north for the rest of the winter, and Ed kept his son entertained with picture letters.

My dear TEDDY-boy. Ottawa, Feb. 7th '36
This morning I saw

Lots of boys and girls having a ride on a big sleigh.

They were going out for a picanic in the woods. They put blankets on the horses to keep them warm and made a big fire on the snow to keep themselves warm Lots of love from DADDY

116

CHAPTER SEVEN

Amos Airways Carries Them All— Promoters, Prospectors and Prostitutes

Although fur-buying missions made up most of Burton's trips, he encountered dozens of gold prospectors anxious to rush north at the slightest chance of a new find. With tents, axes, blankets and pots, their "outfits" were usually carried in a single load. Canoes too large to fit inside the Curtiss Robin or Fairchild would be tied outside. Blanket-wrapped cases of dynamite were often the last items to go. Generally traveling in pairs, prospectors worked a specific area and then flew out from pre-arranged pick-up spots.

At the office, the fortune hunters would point to a spot on a sun-faded map dotted with pinholes, tears and coffee stains.

"What'll you charge to take us there?"

As a scale, Amos Airways compared most lakes with Revillart Lake. It was small but the pilots knew they could operate safely with full loads. If the destination matched the size of Revillart Lake, they agreed on a price with little haggling and the prospectors squeezed into the heavily-loaded airplanes.

When Burton saw stacks of sample bags during the pick-up flight, he knew these "hard-working optimists," as he described them, had made a find. If deemed profitable, they sold the claim to a mining promoter who in turn developed the property. As a result, a shack town often sprang up almost overnight and cat trains (strings of tractor-pulled sleighs) provided winter freighting. Nevertheless, the miners still depended on air services like Amos Airways for personal transport until the strikes became profitable and communities acquired year round roads.

"On a fifty-six-mile hop, which took me about thirty minutes, my passenger looked down at the unbroken rapids, jagged rocks, tangles of underbrush and fallen timber," said Burton. "He told me the same trip took sixteen hours by snowshoe and dog team."

Burton flew occasional charters from Val d'Or with a flamboyant character known as the "Russian Kid." A giant in size, he staked dozens of claims but seldom carried more than a pair of socks attached to his belt. When not poking under tree roots or dynamiting holes in the ground, he ran a small hotel and developed a reputation for illegal high grading or buying stolen gold from miners for resale.

Once, a stranger arrived at the Russian Kid's hotel and checked in. He asked surreptitiously if anyone would be interested in buying a chunk of gold. The local prospectors and businessmen immediately pegged him as an undercover police officer.

"You won't sell it here," said the Russian Kid. "It's too risky."

"I've got a chunk worth about $3,000 but I'll let it go for a thousand quick cash," the stranger said, knowing the gold would be recovered when he made an arrest.

"Tell you what," the Russian Kid suggested. "There's a fellow at the Lamaque Mine owes me. We'll drive over and get the money and I'll pay you."

During the drive, the Russian Kid kept the truck's window open. "Let me have a look at that rock," he said. The officer handed the gold over to the Russian Kid so he could examine it. At a bend in the road, a man with a dog team and toboggan stood by. Suddenly, the Russian Kid pitched the gold into the snow and slammed down the gas pedal. The man with the dogs scooped up the gold and vanished into the dense bush.

The officer went wild with rage and struggled to turn off the car's ignition. No match for the giant Russian, they continued to the Lamaque Mine.

"So what's the matter with you?" demanded the Kid. "You offered me gold for 1,000 dollars and here it is. Count it. You got your money; I got the gold. If I want to throw it out the window, that's my business."

After the policeman left town and the story of his loss had spread, Burton asked the Russian Kid if he someday planned to return to his homeland.

"I go back to Rooshia when there are no more suckers left in this country," he laughed.

Prospectors who found the bonanza of their dreams frequently went to ridiculous lengths to spend their newly earned wealth. Amos Airways received a radio call from an eccentric individual.

"Mr. Davees, Mr. Davees," the heavily accented voice shouted. "I'm wanting you bring me one case beer in your hairoplan."

"Only one case?" Davis asked. "Our airplanes carry a ton."

"I'm telling you, I want you bring me one case beer," the prospector bellowed.

"But it's going to cost you sixty dollars for us to come out there anyway," Davis insisted. "That's all you want? One case?"

"Look you here, Mr. Davees. I want you bring me one case beer. Anudder time I call you and get you bring me anudder case beer. Now, I want you bring me just one case, that is all."

"Okay," Davis said. "One case of beer."

Eventually, Burton and Davis made several flights to the prospector's shack—each time with one lonely case of beer in the cabin of their "hairoplan."

Gold strikes drew hordes of prospectors to Amos and Rouyn. The provincial government opened a previously closed section of land but staking could begin only after midnight on a specified date. Before the appointed time, Burton and Davis flew all during the daylight hours. One promoter named Edward Deane, having been involved in rushes before, suggested that some caution was needed.

"On one rush, there were so many that night with flashlights and axes, a man was lucky if he didn't have his leg cut off for a stake," he said. "I got out of there while I still had two good legs to walk on."

To maintain legal ownership, every claimant had to make certain improvements within a year of staking. These included erecting a cabin and showing proof of diggings. After the first twelve months, the deadline expired at 7:00 A.M. If the required duties were not performed, anyone could stake the ground.

One morning, a man rushed into the base office, pointed to a spot on the map and demanded an immediate flight. Price did not enter the picture. Burton readied the Curtiss Robin as quickly as he could and soon placed the bulbous nose of the hard-worked freighter on course for the customer's lake. As the shoreline came into view, they saw a canoe bound for the same claim. As Burton banked overhead, the man in the canoe paddled furiously.

"We've got to beat him to it," yelled his passenger. "God, don't let him get there ahead of us."

Luckily, the wind died, leaving the lake calm so Burton could land in any direction. He eased down and skimmed the water close to the lakeshore. Before the floats grounded on the beach, his passenger scrambled through the door with ax in hand and jumped into the shallow water. The other man tumbled from his canoe at the same time and left it to drift. The two splashed to shore, raced up the bank side-by-side and disappeared into the trees.

Within an hour they returned. Both climbed into the airplane to catch their breath and have a friendly chat. Each had successfully staked claims which later sold for $1,000.

Not all interchanges were so cordial. Sometimes, especially at Christmas, when Burton landed at mine sites, up to fifty people with packsacks, suitcases and duffle bags formed a line waiting to go to Amos. The rush to grab a seat often began before the propeller stopped. During a pickup, Burton had already loaded when four men stepped up.

"Look, buddy," one said, "we've been waiting out here for three hours already and gotta catch a train to Montreal. Be a good guy and take us on the next trip, will you?"

Burton promised he would and took off. When he returned, a burly character whipped open the door, climbed in and plunked himself into a seat. The four to whom Burton had promised the next ride stood outside.

"I'm going," the husky man declared. "I been waiting as long as anyone and I ain't going to give up this seat to no one."

Burton explained his promise to take the others first and pointed out that the federal government did not license the Curtiss Robin for five passengers and their goods. The man would have to wait. Reason didn't work. Burton turned to the four standing outside.

"Any of you want to give up your place to this gentleman?" he asked.

"Hell, no," they all shouted. "Why the hell should we? You promised to take us and we're together. Besides, we got just enough time left to catch the Montreal train from Amos."

"Then it's up to you to get him out," Burton said.

They did not need a second invitation. The door slammed back and the four work-hardened miners piled in and grabbed the interloper who held the airplane's cabin frames and kicked madly. They battled nearly fifteen minutes with gouges, curses and flying fists. While Burton watched, the Curtiss Robin rattled as feet and heads thudded into the thin walls. Finally, the trespasser hit the ground and the men pinned him down in the snow.

Burton started the engine as they scrambled into the Robin. With throttle forward, he blasted the tail around for take off. The reject jumped to his feet and took a powerful kick at the fuselage as Burton roared by, putting his foot through the fabric.

Burton flew to Amos, patched the hole and returned with the police. The angry man was not there; he had escaped on a competitor's airplane.

Some prospectors never left the north country. One, who died at Chicobi Lake in his sleeping bag, had been found in the spring by a passing Native. Burton flew in a coroner, priest and the deceased's former partner for the funeral. Lucille also rode along, taking part in the service on the veranda of a fire ranger cabin. Before the priest started, the partner beckoned to a group of passing Indians.

"Come here, you, please," he said. "Come on, we give dis fellow de good send off."

The service was solemn and respectful. Everyone knelt while the priest intoned the last rites. He drew out a fountain pen from his pocket and sprinkled holy water. Later, Amos residents wondered why the body was not taken to town for burial in consecrated ground. Burton told them that the man's last resting place beneath a lakeshore pine provided a much more fitting place for someone who spent his life in the open. The prospector, he believed, would not have chosen a crowded village cemetery.

Before leaving, the dead man's friends asked Ed, as an impartial party, to distribute the few possessions left behind. When he handed the goods around to the men in turn, one item remained—a small, hand-cranked razor blade sharpener. The group agreed that Ed should have it and handed it over. He kept the souvenir for many years.

At times, Burton's dealings with people of the north were amusing. Two ladies arrived from Montreal and marched directly to Amos Airways. They wanted an airplane dispatched to a camp forty miles away and ordered the pilot to bring a certain man to town.

"Who'll pay for this?" asked Burton.

"He will," replied the shorter of the two, described by Lucille Burton as a wiry, little lady. "He's my husband."

"And he's my husband, too," chirped the other. "You bet he'll pay for it."

The man had married them both. While writing to his respective wives, he inadvertently sealed the letters into the wrong envelopes. They had come to town to settle the score.

Frequently, Burton met colorful characters who "escaped" into the north to seek their fortunes. A prospector called Baldy Price acquired a reputation for knowing every pothole and river bottom in Quebec and Northern Ontario. He also kept himself in superb physical condition by disappearing for days with packsack and pick. Baldy, unlike his contemporaries, rarely worked with a partner because he slammed through the forests like a bull moose and few could keep up. Known to "hoist a few," Baldy occasionally attended prospectors' conventions in the south hoping to sell his claims or find financial backers.

Burton encountered Price at a convention in Toronto's Royal York Hotel. A mining man's symbol of success, the historic hotel served as a place where gold claims changed hands and bush airlines found customers. At a session in which a case of whiskey mysteriously appeared and disappeared, Baldy told the gathering about one of his escapades.

A promoter had sensed potential in Baldy's commanding physical presence and natural flair for the dramatic. Impressed, he asked Price to partner with him in the claim-selling business. Baldy declined and pointed out his preference for life in the bush, never in an office.

"Look, you just come along in your bush clothes and bring your pack," said the promoter. "Pack some samples in it, hang on a frying pan, an ax or whatever you take when you're prospecting. I want you to talk to people about rocks."

Baldy decided that maybe a tour in the south would do him some good after all. He was never told to say he had personally staked any claims but people could believe whatever they wanted. Although not asked to lie as they boarded a New York-bound railroad car, Baldy was not to overdo the truth.

"We went first class with berths in the Pullman and club car seats. Eating in the diner looked like it'd be a problem because I had no tie. Hell, I hadn't worn a tie half a dozen times in my life, but the promoter passed his hand over the headwaiter's so it didn't take long for him to forget I wasn't dressed proper.

"We had fine dinnerware, crystal glasses and the best of food. Once in a while, the promoter speaks to some fancy dude and when he had his attention, I'd smile at his lady friend and she'd smile back. I knew right then that proper clothes didn't matter much."

Baldy Price and his well-dressed business partner checked into a modern hotel equivalent to Toronto's Royal York instead of the bug-infested lodgings Price usually patronized. The promoter gave Price $500 and told him to spread it around as if he had found the legendary mother lode.

"I walked across the floor with my pack and frying pan, ax, snowshoes and all, and my feet in the hobnail boots going clickety-click on the marble floor. Everyone sat up and took notice, and some of 'em fancy ladies smiled. I was beginning to like the game."

When a porter tried to pick up Baldy's pack, he could not lift it. As the little man and two bellboys lugged it to an elevator, Price warned them not to drag the tails of his snowshoes on the floor. The porter received a dollar tip and soon, men in tailored suits arm-in-arm with pretty ladies packed the suite. When introduced as "Baldy Price, the man who struck it rich," a costly case of rye appeared and Price tipped the bell boy with a five-dollar bill.

Baldy's promoter friend handed out samples from the north. As the liquor flowed, they told a tale about seeing a quartz vein from the air. Price said he had flown into the Abitibi River area in search of the vein but nearly starved after a bear destroyed his camp.

"I sez, 'It seemed there was nothing like a quartz vein in the whole country, nothing but granite, granite, and more granite.' I tells 'em, 'Everybody knows granite ain't no good,' and they all, even the women, nodded their heads as if they knowed exactly what I was talking about. 'I struck country with a lot of overburden where you couldn't see what was underneath, and a lot of muskeg.' I laid it on real thick about walking through the swamp and how bad the flies was. Then at last, I sez, 'I struck greenstone.'"

Baldy described how he found the greenstone backed up against the granite and there was the gold. To emphasize the find's importance, Baldy sipped his rye from time to time and passed the bottle.

"I told 'em that as soon as I seen what I found, I cut my stakes and drove 'em in. I lost track of the days, but I knew the airplane was due in soon, and you can just bet I was right there when it came. I hightailed it into town and recorded my find."

By the time he finished embellishing the yarn, the New Yorkers bought all the claims. In fact, Baldy said, some tried to get him in a corner by himself to cut out his partner.

"It just goes to show you that there ain't no honor among thieves," he concluded.

Although Baldy Price described the unscrupulous money hungry promoters and backers of New York and Toronto, Burton found northerners to be trustworthy and trusting. He and Davis routinely hauled gold bricks from the mines. Stored in easily broken wooden boxes containing at least $50,000 worth and left in plain sight at both ends of the trip, no one ever stole an ounce. Mine managers simply asked for a signature at pickup and another when Amos Airways' sleigh delivered them to the express office.

In the outlying mining districts, the commercial pilots were often the only contact from "outside." A lady known as "Boxcar Annie" ran a thriving bootleg business from a tiny log building adjacent to the mines. Her nickname came from a dubious establishment she had once run out of a boxcar adjacent to a newly developed mine.

As Boxcar Annie accumulated a fortune, her main desire was to ensure that her daughter would acquire a formal education. When Burton's Robin touched down and his passengers had gone to work, she placed a large sum of money in his hands.

"I want you to pay my daughter's tuition at boarding school and take what's left over to finish off some bills I owe," said Boxcar Annie.

Although Burton told her he was willing, he hesitated to associate the respected name of Amos Airways with a business that, technically, operated on the wrong side of the law.

"Annie, I can't give you a receipt because the police know you're here and who you are," he said. "They're bound to raid your place before long and I don't want them finding a receipt with my name on it or they'll think I'm in the bootleg business."

"I don't expect a receipt and don't want one," replied Boxcar Annie. "I can trust you to help me out."

They sealed the transaction with a drink of fine whisky. This occurred at a time when pilots taking an occasional bottle of beer or downing a short snort was not as severely frowned upon as in later years.

"Annie, I thought you only sold rotgut," said Burton.

"I do, but when I want a drink for myself, I only use the best," she replied.

Burton took the money and never betrayed her trust. Boxcar Annie's daughter went to school.

The north lacked an abundance of female company so ladies from Montreal provided "entertainment" whenever they could. Every bush country air service carried dozens of perfumed young women into mining and lumber camps and after a few days, brought them out, haggard but richer by far. The law, however, insisted on curtailing such activities, as a pretty pair of dubious repute, both about twenty-two years of age, learned a few hours before arriving at Amos Airways skiplane base.

"How much will you charge to take us over to the Siscoe Mine and drop us off?" they asked Burton, who replied that the price was seven dollars and fifty cents each.

"Sounds reasonable but we've only got five dollars," one said. "We just came from court where they soaked me 150 dollars and my little friend here, they soaked her seventy-five dollars and it's only her second offense. If that ain't mean! Just look at these receipts."

She handed over some slips of paper.

"They took all we had and turned us loose with only five bucks between us," the girl said. "Would you run us over for that?"

"Wouldn't pay for the gas," replied Davis. "We'd go broke."

"Tell you what. You take our five dollars, run us to Siscoe and we'll give you the rest as soon as we get there," one said. "We've got lots of friends. We won't keep you waiting."

The proposition sounded like a safe risk so Davis authorized Burton to fly them to a mine in production near Val d'Or. On arrival, one girl snatched his hat and ran up to an expectant crowd of freight handlers, taxi drivers, lumberjacks and miners. The men cheerfully dipped into their pockets and dropped their contributions in the hat. Within five minutes, the ladies returned to the idling Robin and handed over a pile of cash. Burton found that the men had contributed over twenty dollars and offered to return the balance.

"That's okay, kid, it's yours," the girls said. "You trusted us. Lots more where that came from. So long and thanks a million." Not all customers could be taken at their word. Three men had staked a number of claims a 100 miles south of Amos and needed transportation so they could work the ground when the snow cleared. On the office map, they indicated a possible landing spot and climbed into the Fairchild. Without seats or safety belts, they rode where most passengers did in the 1930s—on top of the load.

On this trip, there were few signs of life. Quebec bush pilots estimated that spring breakup would probably take place within a week. In fact, Burton occasionally saw trappers with canoes lashed to their sleighs in case they broke through the thinning ice. As the Fairchild plodded on, one passenger, who had signed the manifest only as Jack, wrenched a bottle of rye whiskey from his packsack and swallowed its contents. While Burton circled to land, Jack passed out. To be certain they were above the correct site, Burton woke him.

"Sure, that's it, right down in this bay," Jack said and fell asleep again.

They landed in the slushy spring snow and two of the men stepped out. Jack, dazed and barely able to stand, leaned against the Fairchild's metal wing strut, nearly bending it.

"Wait a minute, this ain't the place," he slurred.

"It's the spot you showed me on my map," Burton told him. The other two men could not help since neither had been there before.

"I'm telling you, this ain't it," Jack mumbled. "I know the place when I see it and this ain't it. See, here's my claim."

He pointed to a large, wrinkled blueprint. Burton realized instantly that he had been told to land on a different lake. The claims were over a towering hill to the west. Jack and his partners climbed back aboard and Burton opened the throttle for takeoff. With engine at full power, the Fairchild would not budge in the sticky snow. Two men jumped out to shake the wing struts and kick the skis.

Once on the move, Burton dared not stop. He left the pair in the slush and landed on the other lake close to the claim.

Once again, Jack grumbled: "This ain't the place."

By now, darkness was approaching and Burton had reached the limit of his patience. Worse, two men without provisions or even an ax waited back at the original touchdown spot. Burton went over the blueprint a second time, and knew that he had picked the correct location.

"I guess you're right," Jack finally admitted. "I see it now. Over there's where I had my camp." He dragged a tent out of the airplane and promptly fell asleep on it, leaving the packs to Burton to unload by himself.

The knee-deep slush presented a serious problem, even with an empty airplane, and Jack was of no help. Before starting the engine, Burton cut several saplings from the bush and inserted them under the skis. After warming up, he alternated with the throttle wide open and completely closed before breaking loose to take off and retrieve his stranded passengers. When he returned to Amos, darkness forced him into making a tricky night landing on the Harricana River without lights.

The mining and fur industries kept Amos Airways far from bankruptcy but with established roads cutting into the air freight business, flying hours dropped dramatically. The company also lost revenue when Fairchild G-CANB broke through the ice after its fourth trip moving a survey crew into Amos and had to be taken to a factory in Montreal to have the wooden stringers reglued.

Davis had no alternative except to lay off his friend and employee. Burton's last trip took place in the Curtiss Robin on January 20, 1938, when he carried a load of aerial surveyors on a flight to trace mica veins from the air. Never far from aviation, Burton hoped his next job would permit him to continue living in Amos.

CHAPTER EIGHT

By Biplane to the Barrenlands

Instead of lamenting the lack of aviation employment, Burton almost immediately took a position at the Perron Mine, not far from Amos. A "pencil pusher" again, he steadily expanded his knowledge of the mining industry and soon was manager of the mine's general store. Although most airlines and air services struggled to survive, the pilot-turned-storekeeper noticed that more exploration companies and syndicates now began acquiring their own airplanes. One publication described these corporate aircraft as the "medium of northern development."

During a brief visit to Toronto in the spring of 1939, Burton took a hop in a Taylor E-2 Cub and discovered that although he may have been a "little rusty" he still retained his basic skills. Coincidentally, word circulated that an organization called GB Explorers Ltd. needed a pilot who not only flew well but understood the language of geology. Burton, with his Mitchell Expedition background and accident-free experience in Quebec with the mining industry, made an ideal candidate.

Financed by Toronto mining engineers, Glen R. Burge and Murdock Mosher, GB Explorers considered the geologically untouched Northwest Territories as an area of great promise.

They recognized, however, that the short exploration season demanded reliable transportation if they were to stay ahead of ground-bound prospectors.

"At first, they thought about buying or leasing a gigantic twin engine biplane on floats called a Fleet Freighter that had just been built in Fort Erie," said Burton. "The trouble was, it was an untried airplane. After about thirty minutes, I saw that it'd be too cumbersome to park on rocky shorelines and docks weren't too plentiful where they planned to go."

Instead of field testing the huge Freighter, which later failed to attract many buyers, Burge and Mosher leased a 1935 YKC-S biplane produced by the Western Aircraft Company or Waco in Troy, Ohio. Canadian distributor W. J. Sanderson handled the deal on behalf of Fleet Aircraft and on May 25, 1939, Burton flew CF-AWH for the first time.

Pilots considered this elegant cabin biplane to be the "Stutz Bearcat" of the air, after a luxurious automobile, recognized as the epitome of excellence at the time. The twenty-five-foot wing span and stubby fuselage provided a maneuverability matched by few other types. Powered by a 225-hp Jacobs L-4 engine known to the flying fraternity as the "Shaky Jake," the Waco weighed 3,250 pounds loaded and carried 1,000 pounds with pilot and full gas tanks.

Burton's first passengers were his employers' families on sightseeing rides along the Toronto harbor front. The extra hours allowed him to familiarize himself with the Waco's sensitive controls. When not practicing, he arranged living accommodation for Lucille and Teddy in the city. Unfortunately, they would be unable to accompany him to Yellowknife for the summer.

After three days of local flying, Burton put together a kit of tools, spare parts, picks, shovels and other prospecting equipment. He also purchased a lightweight silk tent for emergency use. On June 17, he pumped out the Edo floats and with Burge and Mosher, took off from Toronto's choppy harbor and headed north.

A fuel stop at Sudbury provided a brief break and they continued to Geraldton, 122 miles northeast of Port Arthur/Fort William where they remained for the night. Next day, they landed at Sioux Lookout in a heavy rainstorm. Grounded by poor visibility, they secured the Waco and waited out the weather in a hotel. Three days and nine fuel stops later at outposts like The Pas, Manitoba and La Ronge, Saskatchewan, they touched down beside a rocky peninsula known as Yellowknife, a community named for the Yellowknife Dene Indians who had moved into the area in the 1800s.

Although gold on Great Slave Lake had been known since 1896, it was not until 1936 that the frontier community became a boomtown. Several companies sank shafts, and commercial gold production had only commenced two years before Burton's arrival. No stranger to rushes, Burton marveled at the ingenuity and enterprise encouraged by rumors of more strikes to the north.

"Barges arrived every day from across Great Slave Lake at Hay River," he said. "Wherever we looked, warehouses, wharves and mine headframes were going up and you could hear hammers pounding and saws slicing the huge rafts of timber they floated in. Sometimes, the sky seemed crowded with airplanes skittering back and forth between the camps and town."

With Yellowknife as their base, Burge and Mosher concentrated on hiring prospectors and arranging supplies. Burton, aware that the lightweight Waco had been designed as a sportsman's pleasure craft and not for harsh sub-Arctic and Arctic conditions, fine-tuned the engine. When finished, he carefully inspected every inch of the airframe for cracks and corrosion.

Off duty, he chatted with local pilots who told him that some of the mining activity was based on ore samples handed over by Indians. Members of outlying Dene, Hareskin and other tribes told gold seekers that the "magic metal" had been found in huge veins close to the "big lake." The question was whether the rocks had been picked up at functioning mines or carried on their backs from the wilderness. In any case, few listeners passed up any possibility. They investigated every rumor.

With arrangements made to carry them through the season, including living quarters, Burge and Mosher ordered Burton to begin dropping men into camps selected on the basis of sketchy reports and instinct. Flying outward and away from the volcanic basalt of Yellowknife, Burton saw countless patches of muskeg and conifer-edged pothole lakes crisscrossed by bare rock outcrops. On one trip, he spotted a cluster of men removing overburden and decided to drop down for lunch.

The crew welcomed him and provided a tour of their diggings before he began bringing out his sack of sandwiches. Although the men had finished their meal, the cook stopped him.

"Look, I just threw away the rest of the fish but if you want to wait a minute, I'll get another and whip you up a good feed," the cook offered.

Pleased with the idea of fresh pan-fried trout, but expecting a long wait, Burton saved his sandwiches for another time. The cook slid a canoe into the water, paddled a few feet from shore and dropped a nearly transparent fishing line into the water. Scarcely wet, it twanged seconds later as a glistening eight-pound lake trout slammed into the lure.

"You always get them that fast?" the incredulous lunchtime guest asked.

"Nobody has to go far around here," the cook replied.

Although the terrain over which Burton flew did not match the dead-end canyons, high cliffs and unpredictable winds he had known in British Columbia and the Yukon, he had other hazards to contend with. The area close to Great Slave Lake nurtured tracts of spire-like spruce and dried moss which created a forest fire potential during hot summers. Highly resinous, the slightest lighting bolt or careless match could set them off.

Assigned to move mining engineers to a pothole near Ptarmigan Lake where a crew had stripped away the earth, Burton landed and tied the Waco to shore. Invited to accompany them to the site, he declined, planning to carry out minor maintenance on the oil-burning Jacobs engine. Intent on his work, Burton had nearly completed the inspection when he heard a tremendous express-trainlike roar behind him.

Suddenly, an immense cloud of black boiling smoke billowed over a ridge and down the hill as flames flashed through the moss-floored forest toward the Waco. With barely time to heave the engine covers into the freight compartment, Burton pushed away from shore and jumped inside the cockpit, choking and spluttering in the heat. He hit the starter switch and thankfully, the cantankerous Jacobs caught on the first try. He jammed the throttle forward, slammed the tail into the water and roared across the lake at full power.

At a safe distance, he shut down and waited for the fire to burn itself out. Embers, carried aloft by the heat, hissed into the water but none landed on the Waco's highly flammable fabric covering. From his perch on the wing, Burton watched his passengers groping and stumbling over the singed ground and hot rocks. Expecting to find the airplane reduced to a pile of melted tubing, they were relieved to see CF-AWH silhouetted in the slowly dissipating haze.

"Swift-moving fires like this one weren't unusual in the sub-Arctic near Great Slave," explained Burton. "Camp fires sometimes smoldered over winter in moss under the snow. When spring came, the vegetation dried and flared up with the first strong breeze that came along. Sometimes, the smoke caused us a lot of lost days when I had to sit it out in Yellowknife."

Over the next few weeks, Burton, always interested in natural phenomena, particularly when the subject matter contributed to keeping him alive, familiarized himself with the lay of the land and local weather patterns. Generally, clear skies and light winds predominated and fog rarely formed in spite of the presence of hundreds of lakes and grassy swamps. The trips ranged north of Great Slave Lake for an average of an hour and consisted mainly of "grub and gas." External loads of canoes became routine and rarely did the Waco fly empty.

Some trips took GB Explorers as far north as Great Bear Lake. The landing near Echo Bay marked the farthest north Burton would venture in his lifetime. It was here where Gilbert Labine discovered pitchblende ore in 1930. Near the famous site, rumpled dark hills merged into sheer rock walls reaching straight to the lake shore. One peculiar outcrop called Mystery Island fascinated the party.

Under certain temperature and light conditions, the island seemed to rise out of Great Bear and float. At other times, it sank below the water. According to Indians who trapped and hunted the area, a woman had slipped away from her family to rendezvous with a secret lover on the island. The vengeful husband paddled from the mainland and stole their canoes. Marooned, the lovers starved. Natives believed the island moved when the departed spirits returned. What they saw was a mirage, not uncommon near the cold water lakes of the north. They told prospecting parties that no animals lived there.

From time to time, Burton put aside his flying and mechanical duties to join the ground parties. During an exploratory flight northeast of Yellowknife, he and passengers Mosher and prospector Burt Smith noticed an unusual rock formation. Circling overhead, Burton calculated a compass bearing from the nearest suitable landing place. He touched down in a sheltered narrow bay with black rocks on the right and a low shoreline wooded by feathery larches and white-barked birch. They then faced a three-mile walk over stony ground.

"In places like this, I often thought that no one had ever been there before," said Burton. "Yet, close to where we set up our tent, we found a pile of rotting poles from an old tepee."

134

To cover more area, the group split up and followed different routes to meet at the pond where they had seen the interesting rock formation. Traversing the stony ground proved far rougher than anyone expected. Ridges, which looked like gentle furrows from the air, turned out to be challenging, steep-sided gullies. Nevertheless, Burton arrived ahead of the others, lit a fire and boiled tea for the crew. Although his leg had healed since the 1924 crash, it still pained him when hiking for long periods. In any case, Mosher was impressed that Burton navigated on the ground as well as he did in the air.

After hours of tramping across angled rocks and slippery stones, the party concluded that their samples contained only valueless traces of gold. Quartz veins spread everywhere but nothing seemed worth mounting a major drilling expedition for, much less a future mine.

Although Burton enjoyed the educational aspects of mineral exploration, the men of GB Explorers experienced many disappointing times. While investigating reports and rumors of gold,

the principals realized that few had prospected the vast expanses stretching from Fort Reliance on Great Slave Lake's east end as far as Clinton-Golden Lake and north to the Back River. With the airplane and an experienced pilot like Burton, their chances of success exceeded those of their competitors who were still restricted to a few days' canoe ride from Yellowknife.

With the Waco packed to the ceiling and Burge and Mosher wedged into their seats, Burton staggered it off the water of Yellowknife's Back Bay and turned southeast on July 8, 1939. They had arranged to use fuel that had been shipped in the previous year on a Hudson's Bay Company barge to Fort Reliance.

"The first leg out from Yellowknife coincided with high winds," Burton said. "When we made the 175 miles across Great Slave into McLeod Bay, the waves were strong enough to roll beach boulders back and forth but we found a sheltered spot beside the RCMP barracks and got down without breaking anything."

An RCMP officer named Thompson lived in a trim, whitewashed house adjacent to a workshop crammed with dog harnesses, traps and canvas sheets. Stationed at Fort Reliance for three years with an Eskimo interpreter, Thompson kept his mind and body occupied by doing as much work as possible. Everything he did, he kept to a strict, self-imposed schedule, including polishing anything with a smooth surface and painting and repainting the walkway stones. A house-size pile of wood and nets brimming with freshly caught fish for his dogs attested to his endless efforts.

While helping to fill the Waco's gas tank, Thompson told them they were the first human visitors in three months. Fort Reliance, he explained, served as a gateway to the Barren Grounds. Indians from settlements around Great Slave trapped the shorelines, but since Eskimos resented having Indians enter their territory, RCMP policy discouraged them from traveling further north.

To maintain the peace, it was thought best to keep the two traditional enemies apart as much as possible. British explorer Samuel Hearne had witnessed their mutual hatred during a confrontation in 1771. A party of Chipewyans had massacred a group of sleeping Eskimos caught in their tents. The slaughter was never forgotten by the horrified Hearne, and government people were much aware of the continuing enmity between the two groups in the 1930s.

Two days later, after Burge and Mosher had examined the mineral formations within a few miles of Fort Reliance, Burton readied the Waco for flight. Besides their camping gear, he added several wooden poles. Nothing capable of supporting a tent existed in the Barrens since tree growth became sparse the farther north they flew.

After an hour at 2,000 feet above landscapes speckled with rock clusters shattered by eons of winter cold, Burton noticed a strangely shaped rock formation. Bright red, it jutted out sharply in boulder fields left behind by glacial retreats eons ago. His passengers wanted to land on a nearby slate-colored lake to take samples.

"As there were no trees to tie the airplane to, I picked up a long sliver of rock to bury for an anchor post," Burton said. "Taking a pick and shovel, I began digging. To my surprise, the ground was frozen nine inches down, though it was the middle of July. No wonder the land is barren."

The group confirmed the formation to be slightly east of seventy-mile-long Artillery Lake. They unloaded the Waco and decided to stay for three days. In grounds where vegetation consisted of spindly grass, damp moss and stunted hardwood shrubs, meal times became major projects. Everyone gathered armloads of whatever burnable material they could find to create cooking fires. Caribou trails ran through their camp but, except for occasional jaegers (large dark-colored birds), no animal life seemed to exist.

With sample bags packed for later assay in Yellowknife, they backtracked to Fort Reliance for fuel. After seeing so little sign of wildlife, the airborne prospectors were surprised when, ahead of the airplane's nose, a large mass of brown seemed to ooze over the hills like paint thrown against a sanded door. Dropping lower, the party was astounded to see an enormous herd of migrating caribou.

Shapes of hundreds of animals took form the closer they came. Bulls, with horns looking oversize for their lean spindly bodies, flanked the herd's edge and in the center, light brown yearlings trotted beside their panting mothers. By counting separate groups, Burton estimated over 10,000 animals on the run to their spring feeding grounds. Later, his photographs confirmed the estimate.

At Fort Reliance, Burton joined Constable Thompson as he fed his shaggy huskies. The pups were kept in a small enclosure, half-grown ones in another, and ten mature dogs tethered to stakes growled and slavered when the men approached. Most were white, part-wolf working creatures rather than pets.

"That nearest one's the only one that's safe for you to touch," explained Thompson. "If you want to put a hand on him, never be in a hurry and don't make any quick moves."

The dog allowed Burton to fondle its ears, but showed no response. Thompson added that the dog was one of his best but even he had to be extremely cautious. On sleigh trips, no one, not even his master who fed and cared for him, dared break trail ahead for if the person fell, the animal would immediately attack and tear him to shreds.

Next morning, the party left McLeod Bay again to survey Artillery Lake's rocky shore close to their last camp. Drifting fields of ice blocks hindered landings in many places and on the west end of Clinton-Golden Lake, they saw that solid ice still covered the surface. Open water appeared at Muskox Lake, ninety-eight miles southeast of Contwoyto Lake.

During their inquiries in Yellowknife, Burge and Mosher had heard of a trapper and his son who had been flown north of the treeline and arranged for pickup after they caught their quota of white Arctic fox and wolf. Known to be an amiable pair, they knew the area well and would likely be willing to share their knowledge of the land. Burge decided to make a trip to their cabin at Muskox Lake to meet them.

The Murphys greeted the crew as they disembarked from the Waco in front of a rough, moss-chinked shack hammered together from weathered boards resting on mounds of stones. Caribou skins served as a door and bed sheets formed a primitive curtain to keep out the twenty-four-hour daylight. The sod roof reminded Burton of his homesteading days on the Saskatchewan prairie. "You hit it about right," the older man said. "The ice only went out of this lake about five days ago."

Self-taught, the younger Murphy genuinely enjoyed the isolation. Instead of looking upon the tundra as an arena from which to wrest a living, he studied the creatures and vegetation within it. In a corner of his home, collections of carefully pressed wild flowers contrasted sharply with musty sleeping robes and long expired bacon and bannock. He understood the scientific names of each one. Later, as he and Burton looked over the Barrenlands, he described the hard work they endured just to survive.

"My, but this is grand country; we don't have a neighbor for 150 miles," he said. "We make the trip down to Edmonton once a year for a quick visit, but we're always glad to come back here again."

"What do you do for heat in the winter?" Burton asked when he entered the cabin and noticed a pile of small sticks by the stove. It took several handfuls to heat a kettle.

"We're pretty lucky here," came the answer. "There's a valley a few miles away where we go to dig wood and haul it over with the dogs."

Young Murphy went on to explain that much of their meat supply came from herds of caribou like the rolling mass the Waco flew over several days before. When the animals passed within range of the cabin, they killed only what they needed and watched the others move on. Sometimes, they noticed wolves following and watched them teach their pups how to bring down the frightened caribou. The pair were convinced that the wolves killed for sport, a proposition still debated by wildlife watchers in later years.

Although the father-son team spent two days showing the party where gold might be found, they harbored no resentment of the fact that rich finds would disturb their tranquillity. In any case, nothing came of exploration from Fort Reliance. As payment for their help, the Murphys were dropped off along their trap line and the Waco continued to Yellowknife on July 14.

Burton spent many hours in outlying camps to which he carried food, volatile dynamite, blasting caps and other mining supplies. Occasionally, forest fire smoke reduced flight visibility so that maintaining straight line tracks across countless, similarly shaped lakes and ponds became exercises in masterful map reading. A stop watch, magnetic compass and a well-used notepad were the only navigation tools in the Waco. Nevertheless, Burton never became lost, nor did he run out of fuel. This was a remarkable achievement for the time, when there were absolutely no electronic navigation aids.

Not all flights required intense concentration. On one occasion, after Burge and Mosher learned that an annual treaty payment ceremony would take place at Fort Rae, sixty miles northwest of Yellowknife, they requested the Waco. Speaking with groups of Dogrib Indians who knew the country intimately might provide them with more information on potential gold prospects. After takeoff, Burton only needed to keep his left wing over Great Slave's shoreline. Despite forest fire smoke and low visibility, he couldn't miss the village thirty minutes later.

A point where travel routes from traditional hunting areas converged, Fort Rae was located on Marian Lake, ten miles from the North Arm of Great Slave. In 1852, Hudson's Bay Company explorer Dr. John Rae established a trading post where a substantial Native settlement eventually developed. When the Waco arrived overhead, the Dogribs were camped on a rocky peninsula near the post.

"The lake was very shallow but we were told that the deeper channel was marked with stakes," Burton said. "When we landed, the water was too rough to see the rocks and the Indians had fish nets all around with marking stakes sticking up so it was impossible to tell where the channel might be."

While waiting beside the tethered Waco, Burton drew pen and ink sketches of the curious Indians who came to see the white man's double winged bird. The older men had their hair bound with brightly colored scarves. The black hair protruded straight up, looking much like smoke coming out of a chimney. By the time he finished sketching, Burge and Mosher had completed their inquiries.

The return trip to Yellowknife made him wish he had never left Fort Rae. An exceptionally large forest fire west of Marian Lake produced enough smoke to cause a darkness unusual in the twenty-four-hour Arctic daylight. Without maps, Burton dropped to a few feet above the water and followed Great Slave's shoreline home.

Burton's most unexpected trip took place on August 16, 1939, when he was asked to take GB Explorers' "top brass" to Edmonton. With Mosher and managers Arnold Hoffman and Fred Thompson aboard, they flew across the widest part of Great Slave Lake, picked up the Slave River and followed its meandering, mud-colored coils to Fort Smith.

"We landed at Smith for gas after two hours and then headed for the west end of Lake Athabasca where we followed the Athabasca River to Fort McMurray and landed at the famous snye where a lot of Arctic first flights started from," Burton said. "We still weren't finished so after more gas, made it a little under three hours later to Edmonton—perfect all the way."

Burton toured the city while waiting five days for Mosher and his colleagues to conclude their business. On the return to Yellowknife, they retraced the same route. When the Waco circled Back Bay for landing, the total trip had taken fourteen hours and twenty-five minutes.

"Pleasant—no weather, maintenance or navigation problems," Burton noted in his logbook.

The end of the Northwest Territories' summer season was marked by repetitive snow squalls and plunging temperatures. Burge ordered his pilot to begin bringing in the crews from the

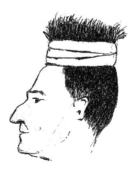

Barrenlands but an unexpected warm spell allowed another "three grand days prospecting." While Burge and Mosher helped prepare for departure, word spread that England and France had declared war on Germany on September 1. Canada followed suit two days later.

On September 6, a group of weather-worn prospectors, bush pilots and Indians watched Waco CF-AWH take off from Yellowknife for the last time. Bound for southern Ontario's greenery, Burton and Mosher (Burge had preceded them by surface transport) stopped at Fort Smith for fuel and then continued a series of hops plagued by low ceilings, snow and rain.

Except for time out to join a bear hunt in Lac du Bonnet, Manitoba, forty-eight miles northeast of Winnipeg, they flew directly to Toronto. On September 14, Burton signed the Waco back to Fleet Aircraft Ltd. and ended his participation in another gold-seeking expedition.

GB Explorers Ltd. continued prospecting and developing several holdings until 1948 when the company charter expired. As for Burton, his uncanny handling of the tiny, easily upset Waco and survival without damage when larger airplanes crashed, disappeared or sank, ranked as an aviation miracle. After being away from Lucille and Teddy for nearly three months, he boarded his family on a train for Florida where they spent the winter on a relative's orange grove. On his return in January, 1940, he applied for enlistment to the nearest RCAF recruiting office in Toronto.

Again, the military turned Burton down. This time, they considered him too old to serve his country.

CHAPTER NINE

Northern Ontario's Fires and Fish

When the RCAF did not take advantage of Burton's experience, he applied to and was accepted by the Ontario government. Reorganized from the original OPAS to the Air Service Division of the Ontario Department of Lands and Forests, and managed by director George Ponsford, the new organization sought high time pilots. Most younger men had volunteered for military service.

Planting fish fingerlings in serene lakes, hauling policemen to Native reserves, doing air ambulance mercy flights along with other useful tasks made a pilot's life with the "Department" an exciting one. The principal drawback, Burton noted, was the regular winter layoffs.

He had the option of winter work in the Lands and Forest hangar at Sault Ste Marie and this he accepted for several seasons. However, in the off months he preferred taking other flying jobs when they were available. Nonetheless, he jumped at any chance to fly the "Yellow Birds," as the provincial fleet had been nicknamed.

On May 9, 1940, Ponsford and Burton climbed into an elegant Stinson SR-9 at Air Service headquarters in Sault Ste. Marie for a familiarization flight. Registered CF-OAY, the Marysville, Michigan-built seaplane had been a luxury type favored by Hollywood movie stars. It cruised at 120 miles per hour and carried at least a 500-pound payload with full fuel. Powered by a 440-hp Pratt & Whitney radial engine, the SR-9, also known as the "Gull Wing" was the most luxurious airplane Burton had ever flown.

Assigned to Red Lake with Stinson CF-BGN for his first summer contract, Burton left "The Soo" with Lucille and Teddy on May 22 and landed two hours and fifteen minutes later at government air base Pays Plat on Lake Superior's north shore. After refueling, they continued to Sioux Lookout where his family transferred to Hamilton CF-OAJ for the final leg to Red Lake. Burton followed several days later with a load of department staff. No roads to the friendly mining community existed and supplies came by air from Kenora, eighty miles southwest, or from Sioux Lookout, ninety-two miles southeast.

The next morning, Burton walked a few yards from his new home on Forestry Point to a pine board dock where mechanic Walter Davidson kept CF-BGN ready to fly. Almost immediately, the unprecedented warm weather sparked a Stinson dispatch to a blaze on nearby MacKenzie Island. Luckily, firefighting crews quickly extinguished the first fire of the season. Veteran forestry staff considered early blazes a sign of busy days ahead.

In conversation with chief ranger Robert Taylor, Burton learned that smoke detection flights would be flown daily. To save time and prevent the loss of valuable timber, Taylor assigned firefighters to ride in the Stinson. This, it turned out, became an innovation brought about by the SR-9's large cabin. Until then, airplanes such as the smaller de Havilland Moth had served only as spotters. Now, the Stinson handled several firefighters and equipment on patrol.

"We'd often head out to Indian reserves to hire firefighters," Burton said. "We'd circle the village, land, shut down and drift near shore. The fire boss would give a few blasts on his whistle and the Indians rushed to their canoes. The first ones to reach us were hired."

After dropping off his charges at fire campsites, Burton returned several times to the reserves until every male capable of holding a shovel had been signed on. Burton often carried boats or canoes on the Stinson's float so crews could travel waterways to attack hot spots from all sides. As flames consumed mature forests and flare-ups threatened hard-earned boundaries, men struggled continuously to contain the main blazes and kept Burton busy from early morning until dark. In Northwestern Ontario, daylight lasted from 6:00 A.M. until 10:00 P.M. in midsummer.

Some fires dragged on for weeks. Heavy smoke threatened communications and frustrated fire bosses joked about ordering cowbells so crews could hear each other. Sometimes, the speed of rampaging flames drove firefighters into the shelter of poplar stands which did not burn as easily as the coniferous softwoods.

Many Native firefighters, pleased to earn money away from traplines and fishnets, brought their cultural beliefs to the firelines. During one severe session, tribal medicine man Joseph Pisk decided to use his powerful magic to slow down the fires. He walked to an unburned lakeshore and faced west with arms across his chest. After meditating and chanting, he rejoined his fellow Indians.

"I bring rains," he announced, solemnly. "Every man go to other end of portage and put two-dollar bill on tree."

Impressed, the exhausted, soot-covered firefighters complied. That evening, a heavy rain inundated the area and snuffed every flame. The next morning, Burton noticed that the soggy two-dollar bills had disappeared.

At the end of each pay period, the Department of Lands and Forests called upon Stinson pilots to fly in clerks who paid the firefighters in cash. Because of the cost of bushplanes and lack of airstrips, few white women visited the remote villages. On one trip, Burton received permission to take his family to Pikangikum.

After the Stinson's floats eased gently past submerged boulders and into the soft sand beach near the Hudson's Bay store, village men helped secure it with ropes. Indian women in bulky woollen sweaters, long brown-ribbed socks and ankle-length skirts watched. Partially covered in colorful shawls, they giggled when the strange white lady dressed like a man stepped ashore. A few of the braver ones edged close enough to touch Lucille's jodhpurs.

"They want to know if she's really shaped like that or if it's the stiff cloth," explained a settlement missionary. "They're laughing because they have never seen a woman in men's clothes and call Lucille *Sparshiganeenaweewan* which means 'the-flying-canoe-man's-wife.'"

Burton encouraged Lucille to travel with him whenever possible. A university graduate and journalist, she took a special interest in Canada's Native people. On one occasion, they landed at Gull Bay on the west side of Lake Nipigon and asked the Hudson's Bay factor, known to the Ojibway as Pootawchie (round like a barrel) where the village's oldest woman lived.

Lucille learned that Mrs. Wigwash enjoyed smoking so she purchased a plug of McDonald's chewing tobacco and another one for smoking.

With a guide, they found her in a soot-streaked lean-to, part of a hand-hewn timber shack that belonged to relatives. Mrs. Wigwash sat on a damp, dirt floor near a tiny fire contained in a blackened metal can. The dingy, unfurnished room smelled of wet earth, unwashed clothing and spruce smoke.

The old lady, shrouded in a blanket so ancient its edges unraveled in long strings, inclined her whitened head toward the door. Age showed in the lines crisscrossing her pocked face and clouded eyes testified to blindness caused by sitting close to smoldering fires all her life. A dimpled tin bowl of porridge rocked as she dipped long yellow fingers into it. A scruffy dog with chewed ears and docked tail shared the meal. The guide, who was her grandson, stated her age as 117 years.

The woman recognized a friendly voice and warmly received Lucille's tobacco. As firelight flickered on spider webs lacing the soot-thickened logs, Lucille pressed a white lace handkerchief into her leathery hands. Mrs. Wigwash's knurled fingers closed over the delicate cloth. In spite of a jaw stiffened by arthritic pain, she smiled and muttered an acknowledgment in Ojibway. Lucille's mutual good will toward Mrs. Wigwash transcended language barriers. A few weeks later Ted Jr., then twelve, met the old lady when on his first paid job fighting a nearby forest fire. He took refuge in her lean-to for a few hours while the villagers held a square dance and drank home brew in the main room. "It was an experience," he said, "but I wouldn't recommend it to anyone today, more than a half century later." The old lady died in that summer of 1944.

In 1941, Ponsford transferred Burton to a seaplane base three miles east of Fort Frances. Here, he flew another Stinson on duties similar to those he had enjoyed in Red Lake. With Stinson CF-BGM, he spent many hours in Quetico Park, an 1,800 square mile wilderness set aside for protection since 1909.

Park rangers monitored the tourists and often endured severe hardships during their patrols. In one case, chief line ranger William Darby sent Burton to a small pond near the Ojibway reserve of Lac La Croix at the park's southwest corner. Unable to land, he selected a larger lake and landed, paddled a canoe down-river to a cabin and loaded a ranger's decomposing body which had lain undiscovered for weeks. Alone and without contact with park headquarters, the man had succumbed to a heart attack.

On another occasion, Burton flew a grub order to a cabin but the towerman did not come to greet him. He began walking the trail to the tower and came upon the man's mangled body. The black bear that had done the deed lay a few yards away in the bush with the towerman's knife protruding from its belly. Ted, Jr., who had volunteered to unload airplanes, remembers being told to leave the dock while the unsightly corpse was transferred to a hearse, and receiving a licking when he did not move fast enough.

BEAR CACHE

147

Known for his extensive flying boat experience, Burton was asked to fly a Vickers Vedette at Orient Bay, north of Nipigon, for the 1942 season. A pusher type similar to but smaller than the Curtiss HS-2L, it had a cedar plank hull with laminated elm frames. The Department of Lands and Forests model was equipped with a 420-hp Pratt & Whitney pusher engine between the wings and cruised ninety miles per hour.

With eighty-three gallons of gasoline, pilot and equipment, the Vedette had a theoretical 242-pound payload. Once, however, Burton struggled to get airborne with himself and four adult passengers. Occasionally, mechanic David Fleming cleared masses of drag-producing wild rice stalks from the hull after landing at Orient Bay.

Burton's duties with Vedette G-CAND included supply flights, fire patrols and checks on the blind spots of lookout towers. On a supply trip, Burton took along Major Stroud, an elderly civil servant close to retirement. The major found the noise of the open cockpit Vedette almost overwhelming in spite of the tight-fitting leather helmet supplied to passengers. At day's end, the Major complained about his damaged hearing.

"That's the noisiest damn airplane I've ever been in," he groaned. "It was terrible and I'm deaf as a post; can't hear a thing now!"

In a faint whisper from several feet away, Burton asked him: "Major, would you like a bottle of beer?"

"By God, don't mind if I do," came the answer.

So much for deafness, Burton thought.

Pilots found Vedette handling qualities pleasant and enjoyed short takeoffs, excellent crosswind capabilities and high rates of climb. Built in 1928 by Canadian Vickers in Montreal, age began to take a toll on its reliability. Orient Bay mechanic Fleming worked tirelessly to keep the airplane flyable. However, no one, not even the engineers in Sault Ste Marie, could predict the engine problems which lay in wait for a Vedette registered as G-CAND.

On May 31, 1944, with radio technician Ev Gordon and tower observer Richard Phillips, Burton left Orient Bay at 3:15 P.M. to track north into Lake Nipigon to repair lookout tower radios.

Thirty minutes later near Kelvin Island, the engine began running rough and threatened to stop. Burton landed immediately, turned off the switches and drifted into a sheltered bay. While checking for broken sparkplug wires or ignition leads, he found a cracked cylinder.

"It wasn't possible to tell how far the break extended without removing the cowling ring, but it appeared to be mostly on the exhaust side and was held in place by the valve spring," Burton said. "When the engine ran, the latter would vibrate considerably over the cylinder head."

Burton attempted taxiing five miles to a deputy ranger base on Jackfish Island but could not maintain direction without using the throttle to blast the engine. Winds and rollers increased and placed the Vedette in a dangerous position. If the engine stopped completely, a northeast breeze would force them into rough water and swamp the airplane. Cautiously, Burton headed for one of the last protected islands.

The trio built a huge moss-fed fire to attract help but gale force winds flattened the smoke. They had no alternative except to overnight in a small tent. In the morning, they ate dehydrated beef from the emergency rations. This vile concoction was, in reality, commercially made pemmican. As the unhappy group peered from the damp, overcrowded shelter, they saw that the winds had not abated.

From their position, the men watched a Stinson SR-9 Reliant and Hamilton Metalplane searching for them. Unfortunately, the island kept the Vedette hidden and the searchers continued on north. Burton, worried they might not be rescued for days, used his time wisely.

He removed the faulty cylinder, piston and rod and capped the hole in the crankcase with a cover whittled from the Vedette's floorboards. Luckily, the offending cylinder had not been the master one on which all others depended. After four days, the north wind finally waned and shifted to a southerly direction. Burton loaded his passengers—now ill from tainted pemmican— and taxied fifty miles to Orient Bay. Burton, accustomed to the hardships of the bush flying trade, recuperated after several days at home but Gordon and Phillips needed emergency medical attention in Port Arthur for food poisoning.

Later, while patrolling Lake Nipigon again, a piece of exhaust stack separated from the old Vedette's engine and flew back through the propeller. A fragment of the blade penetrated the top deck and another lodged in the hull. Vibration threatened to shake the engine from its mounts so Burton quickly reduced power.

"This only made things worse so I shoved the throttle to the stop and at the higher engine rpm, the vibration smoothed out. "By the time I figured things out, we were within gliding distance of Obonga Lake (nineteen miles southwest of Armstrong) so we deadsticked into the waves. The next thing I knew, water came pouring in through this hole in the bottom I didn't know about."

Frantically, Burton and passenger chief ranger "Doc" Gerrard paddled to shore to ground the Vedette. Luckily, the sloping beach prevented the fuselage from sinking to cockpit level and damaging the primitive electric system. Stranded again, Burton went to work to see what he could improvise to return to Orient Bay. Gerrard was not impressed with airplanes in general, and crumbling Vedettes in particular.

"He said: 'Now's the time to get rid of this thing, Ed. Let's let 'er sink.' He handed me the ax to make the hole bigger but I patched the thing up and refloated it and eventually flew back," Burton recalled.

Northern Ontario provided ideal habitat for beaver, a fact appreciated by almost everyone except timber companies and railroads. Dams built by the buck-toothed creatures frequently flooded access roads and rail beds. One road crew destroyed a dam and placed a "Bump" sign beside the depression it had caused in the highway. Next morning, they discovered the structure had been repaired by the family of beavers inhabiting a nearby lodge. The bump sign formed part of the rebuilt dam. Relocating the animals, the men decided, would be the only solution.

Conservation officers live-trapped beaver in gigantic devices which snapped around each animal like a wire suitcase. At Kenora, a pair of adults, two yearlings and two kits, were loaded for Big Island at the south end of Lake of the Woods. Burton landed adjacent to a swamp drained by a stream between a pair of small hills. Nutritious poplar lined the banks and made excellent dam building material.

Burton stopped the engine of his huge yellow airplane, allowed it to weathercock into wind and grounded it on the beach. A conservation officer dragged the cages down onto the float and unfastened the doors. The older animals plunged into the water and reappeared after swimming a safe distance. The kits, however, tried to climb back into the airplane. Petted and pampered in captivity, they had no intention of leaving the comforts of a warm aerial home but, finally, the conservation officer pushed them off the float and they swam after their parents.

The following year, Burton diverted from his fire patrol to swing over Big Island. Circling above a new swamp glittering through the poplar canopy, he knew the beavers had survived. Before returning to his route, he noticed a huge lodge of sticks and a carefully crafted dam at the exact place where the creatures had been released.

In 1945, Ontario's Lands and Forests Air Service Division acquired an airplane type which would serve the organization until 1952. The Noorduyn Norseman, designed by Robert B. C. Noorduyn, made its maiden flight on November 14, 1935, at Montreal. Canadian-designed and the first bushplane produced with flaps, the pug-nosed freighter became synonymous with northern flying. During the war years, most went only to military services in the United States and Canada. Even the Ontario government, which protected the wilderness as part of the war effort, had difficulties acquiring new or used Norsemen.

After a stream of correspondence between Sault Ste Marie, Ottawa and Noorduyn Aviation Ltd. officials, Ponsford arranged to have two U.S. Army Norsemen diverted from the Montreal assembly lines. They functioned so well on forestry duties that the Lands and Forests soon ordered new lighter models called Mark Vs.

Burton picked up Norseman CF-OBG at Sault Ste Marie and ferried it to his Orient Bay base on July 1, 1945. He soon learned that the "Thunder Chicken" as later pilots nicknamed it, carried loads as high as 2,165 pounds with two full 105-gallon gasoline wing tanks, pilot and equipment. The Norseman accommodated bulky loads associated with fish management projects, especially when biologists requisitioned Burton to fly eggs and fingerlings into hundreds of lakes.

"In the first stage, we'd take in a netting crew who stripped the fish of eggs, fertilized them with milt squeezed from the males, returned them to the water and then put the eggs on trays at the hatchery," he explained. "One tray held up to 60,000 pickerel eggs. As they matured, eyes would appear and when they were ready to survive, they'd be scooped in trays crated with ice and loaded into the Norseman."

After landing, Burton stopped the engine and drifted while technicians transferred the eggs into a lake. The moment they contacted the water, tiny fish snapped to life and wriggled away. In later years, larger fingerlings were successfully dropped from overflying airplanes, a technique developed by Burton and other government pilots.

Frequently, wildlife biologists needed air transport for deer surveys. Burton dropped men onto a lakeshore early in the morning and picked them up before nightfall. On one occasion, a solitary biologist boarded CF-OBG after spending his day tramping and studying a small island. Pleased with his findings, he willingly answered Burton's questions about deer numbers.

"Very much overpopulated," the biologist announced. "There must be at least 500 deer on this island. They're going to clean off all the vegetation here and die of starvation pretty quick."

Burton, remembering the masses of caribou during his Barren Land flying, did not understand how 500 animals could exist on a tiny, water-locked island.

"So, how'd you figure that out?" he asked.

"By their droppings and the browsings," came the answer.

"So, how many times does a deer drop in a day?" Burton inquired.

"Well, nobody's quite sure of that," explained the biologist. "We have to do more research. As a matter of fact, I'm thinking of doing a thesis on that very thing."

As to why anyone would base his life's work searching for deer droppings, Burton could not imagine. Nevertheless, deer scat studies later became a more refined science. No other biologists, however, ever estimated such a large population for so tiny an island.

Burton occasionally became involved in more unpleasant work. Commercial air services avoided flying dead bodies and left the gruesome task to government pilots. Burton remembered transporting a two-day-old corpse from Minaki, sixteen miles northwest of Kenora. The body rode upright behind him in the Norseman's cabin. He also helped remove a long-dead trapper from a cabin and in another incident, spent nine anxious days searching for a missing four-year-old girl. Sadly, the efforts of policemen and bushwise trackers from White Dog Reserve, fourteen miles north of Minaki, were in vain. When the child was found, she was dead. Burton flew the child's pitiful remains to Kenora.

In another case, Burton landed at a Lake Nipigon fire tower cabin and became concerned when the towerman did not greet the Norseman. Inside the log building, he found him in a pool of blood on the floor. The man was one of the two with whom he had shared the rotten pemmican.

"He'd been cutting down a tree and omitted to take the precaution of trimming off the lower branches before starting," Burton explained. "One of them caught his ax as he was striking and turned it down, causing him to cut a deep gash in his foot."

The ranger had dragged himself inside the cabin where he collapsed and waited in terrible pain for the Norseman's regular grocery run several days later. Burton cut away the man's boot with a kitchen knife and removed the blood-soaked sock to reveal a ghastly slice between the toes and ankle. Instead of applying a tourniquet, Burton remembered a technique he learned in the Quebec bush.

He returned to the Norseman for a sack of cooking flour. Opening it, he scooped a nestlike depression in the middle, inserted the ranger's foot, packed more flour around the seeping wound, tied the bag on firmly, then dragged the groaning man into the airplane. After stopping at Orient Bay for fuel, he flew on to Port Arthur where an ambulance stood by at a dock near the city's main hospital.

Later, a doctor informed the Lands and Forests office that he did not enjoy clearing the flour-fouled mess from his patient's foot. Nevertheless, he conceded that Burton's innovative efforts saved the man's life.

In 1946, Burton's last season at Orient Bay, a provincial Royal Commission for the study of remote forestry requested a long-range airplane. The itinerary included Moosonee near James Bay and northwest along Hudson Bay to Fort Severn. Ponsford sent Burton with CF-OBG to Port Arthur on July 16 to meet five passengers arriving by train from Toronto. With suitcases and research equipment stacked to the ceiling, Burton flew east to Remi Lake and then north to Moose Factory.

At "Moose" the Hudson's Bay Company factor welcomed the group warmly. While enjoying dinner, a member of the Bay staff joined them. He had not seen the Norseman arrive and assumed the newcomers had dropped in after a trip on the Polar Bear Express, the railroad train which brought tourists to the north country from Cochrane. The commission officials were all informally dressed.

"We heard we were supposed to expect some kind of party to arrive in charge of a colonel or general or some big shot like that," the man snarled. "I'll bet they never get here; brass hats like comfort too much to come to a place like Moose Factory."

The good-natured group, relaxing far away from their high pressure offices, laughed at the man's embarrassment when he learned the identity of his lunch mates.

Next day, Burton paralleled CF-OBG's nose with the lowlands, muskeg swamps and spruce bogs of the west shore of James Bay. After a brief stop at Fort Albany, they rounded Cape Henrietta-Maria and followed Hudson Bay's coastline to Fort Severn, 446 miles northeast of Red Lake. To outsiders, the tumbledown buildings and gumbo mud of Ontario's most northerly settlement appeared bleak. However, Hudson's Bay Company factor Harry Moore and his wife "Margy" firmly believed that Fort Severn stood out as a beautiful place to live.

"Where else would you find such a fine Post as mine?" Moore asked. "We have white whales at the mouth of the Severn River, bears along the coast and always, large flocks of wild geese. What's more, a British field marshal comes to call on me with an airplane!"

Moore showed his visitors a guest book with the signature of "Alexander of Tunis," Canada's governor-general from 1946 to 1952. The third son of the British Earl of Caledon, he had played a major role in the Middle East during World War II when British troops drove German forces back to Tunisia. Although Burton enjoyed such tidbits of history, he never learned the results of the costly commission.

Wildlife officials always preferred the roomy Norseman for trips to communities north of the railroad line. Their many goals included educating Cree and Ojibway bands on wildlife conservation and forest fire prevention. Regional forester Keith Atcheson had summoned them to an open-air meeting at Pikangikum. Speaking in short, unhurried sentences through an interpreter, he told the Indians that camp fires should be completely extinguished. The chief argued that forest fires meant jobs and jobs meant money.

"You let fires get away—no trees, no furs, no money," countered Atcheson. "You put fires out, you have many big trees. Later, lots of beaver. Make more *shu-nee-a* (money)."

Another Lands and Forests spokesman stressed that trappers should leave breeding stock when harvesting beaver. Setting snares far from the lodges increased the capture rate of larger animals and younger ones were left alive. To make his point, the speaker laid out wooden matches to demonstrate how beaver populations increased each year if allowed to breed.

"Big beaver, big money!" he emphasized.

Next, the group flew fifty miles northeast to Deer Lake and set up a movie projector. Word spread rapidly through the village that the white man's strange machine showed spirits. Canoes arrived from all directions for the showing and free trader Oscar Lindokken stood by to interpret.

The film, which dealt with economical trapping practices, opened with a man on the screen drying his furs beside a fire. To the Natives who had never been exposed to moving pictures, the most amazing sequence turned out to be one in which the star set his snare in a pond, caught a beaver, skinned and cured his catch—all within five minutes. Later, footage of an oncoming railroad train rushing toward them astonished and startled the watchers. Many yelled and leaped aside to avoid being run over by the raging black monster.

On August 16, 1947, de Havilland test pilot Russell Bannock made the first takeoff of an airplane that would profoundly affect the Lands and Forests. An immediate success, the Beaver entered Ontario's air arm and began replacing the aging fabric-covered Stinsons and Norsemen. Buhls, de Havilland Moths and metal-fatigued Hamiltons had already been phased out of service.

Burton continued flying the heavy-duty Norseman after transferring to Kenora. He finally tried Beaver CF-OBX on October 23, 1949, and enjoyed the feather-light controls of the new Canadian bushplane. Although he respected the robust Norseman, he was pleased to ferry CF-OBX to Kenora in the spring of 1950. He spent the rest of his career in the marvelous, nearly maintenance-free craft.

The Beaver's versatility allowed the development of many innovations in forest fire prevention and suppression. Special racks allowed the carriage of long loads such as steel poles and lumber. Lands and Forests technicians and pilots also designed a unique system in which forty-pound paper bags of water could be dropped on forest fires. Perilously low over the flames, the pilot pulled a lever to release a row of bags along a small conveyor and out a belly hatch. Burton considered the method ineffective since the paper fed the fire and direct hits on hot spots actually scattered embers.

Later, mechanics attached modified forty-five-gallon containers to each Edo float. The pilot touched down, taxied on the step to fill the tanks with water, then released the load onto the flames. Burton sometimes participated in cargo-dropping from seventy-five feet above the forest canopy. A rip cord attached to the airframe opened the parachute after it passed through a hole in the belly.

"We also 'free-dropped' things like fire hoses or shovels without chutes," he said. "It wasn't unusual for the men on the ground to dig these things out of the muskeg. We became very accurate; once, we hit a water pump with a hose bag and smashed it."

During the early phases of Burton's career with the department, he flew whatever airplane was available. Exceptionally versatile, he understood the limitations of each one and only once, refused to fly a Vickers Vedette assigned to him by Ponsford. A tired relic in danger of falling from the skies and the last of its kind, the obsolete flying boat no longer could be considered dependable. The Vedette's engine was sold and installed in a Sikorsky pusher airplane but failed catastrophically after eight hours of flying. Burton's outright refusal to risk his passengers netted him a partial season in a two-seat de Havilland Moth registered G-CAPA.

Although Burton's logbook showed many hours in Moths, the seaplane version at first presented him with some difficulties. On floats, the propeller had to be swung by hand from behind the blades; his stiff leg made this practice awkward. The extra time taken to climb up and slide over the wing and then climb into the cockpit could be hazardous as the airplane taxied with no one at the controls. For safety's sake, mechanic David Fleming installed extra cut-off switches on the side of the fuselage to kill the engine if the Moth swung toward a shoreline before he regained control.

"I'd always considered the Moth delightful to fly but it could be a handful on windy days, especially when dodging thunderstorms," he said. "Finally, I had the so-called honor of taking the Vedette on its last trip to Sault Ste Marie and returning with a Fairchild 71C. This one, I kept for two seasons before getting a Norseman."

Usually, Lands and Forests pilots signed on for the seaplane season only. After returning their airplanes to Sault Ste Marie for winter reconditioning or storage, they were obliged to fend for themselves. In Burton's case, he was not always satisfied to wait out the cold weather in the comfort of his home but chased down whatever flying he could to remain active.

In December, 1941, for example, he taught navigation and instrument flying to allied pilots from all nations in de Havilland Tiger Moths at Oshawa's #20 Elementary Flying Training School. In the spring of 1942, he answered Ponsford's call but at freeze-up, returned to the RCAF briefly to fly navigation exer-

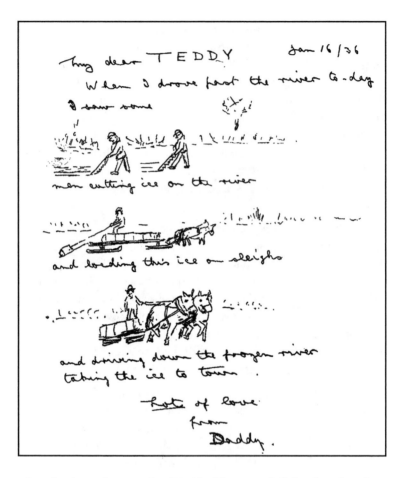

My dear TEDDY   Jan 16/36

When I drove past the river to-day
I saw some

men cutting ice on the river

and loading this ice on sleighs

and driving down the frozen river
taking the ice to town.

Lots of love
from
Daddy.

cises in Avro Ansons for #4 Air Observers' School at London,
Ontario.

January, 1943, marked Burton's reentry into mail flying. He
accepted a winter contract with Leavens Brothers Air Service to
pilot a British-built 130-hp three and a half seat de Havilland Fox
Moth with the lettering CF-API. Lucille and Teddy joined him to
live in Leamington, twenty-three miles southeast of Windsor. The
work bore no resemblance to the hectic, dangerous days and
nights of 1931. Instead, he flew CF-API on Canada's shortest
mail run (fourteen miles) from Leamington across Pigeon Bay to
Pelee Island on Lake Erie. His logbook showed 101 crossings.

"The water between the island and the mainland seldom froze solid since there was too much current," said Burton. "Pheasants were plentiful and protected but the residents sometimes showed their appreciation of our service by slipping a brace of birds into my mail compartment before takeoff."

Although the farmers enjoyed doing what they could for Leavens Brothers pilots, their intentions were not always appreciated. Once, when Burton left the Fox Moth to arrange a load of freight, a farmer decided to help by starting the engine on his own. With too much throttle, the airplane roared away at full power, ran along the ground, careened out of control and went up on its nose. Burton had a shattered propeller and cracked fuel tank to explain to his bosses who were headquartered in Toronto.

After World War II, Burton became fulltime staff in Sault Ste Marie and spent several nonflying off seasons in the Air Service hangar as an office hand or paint shop helper. In 1955, he entered in Pilot's Log Book #9: "Stayed at Kenora through Winter." With 7,900 hours in his logbook, he flew his final summer on Beaver CF-OBX the same year and settled with his family in the friendly tourist community on Lake of the Woods.

Retired, Burton finally had time to search for the answers to questions his curious mind had pondered over the years. He delved heavily into philosophy and according to son, Ted, picked up an annoying habit of marking books and bending corners. Restless and unaccustomed to so many leisure hours at his island home on Lake of the Woods, Burton took a job as a bookkeeper for Kenora's Co-op Dairy.

His supervisor for that period was a man he had twice flown out from bush camps with polio. Before vaccine became available, most commercial air services refused to carry passengers afflicted with the dreaded disease. It often fell to Lands and Forests pilots to carry out mercy missions. Although some refused, Burton never hesitated.

During his retirement, he drew upon personal notes and recollections to complete an autobiographical manuscript started years earlier. It was a labor of love as he relived and recounted the sights, sounds and adventures of his younger years.

On January 14, 1957, he reported to a local doctor for a routine medical exam and learned that his pilot's license would be canceled. It came as no surprise, however, for Burton had known his deteriorating eyesight could never be corrected with glasses. During his last year of flying, distortions in his vision made it necessary for him to cover one eye when landing.

Burton ventured back into the air only rarely. His last trips occurred when he volunteered to travel to the ice-locked shore of Hudson Bay as a navigator for a pilot who was unfamiliar with the nightmarish labyrinth of lowland lakes and swamps that make up the area.

Until his flying certificate lapsed for medical reasons, Edward Cherry Burton held the honor of being Canada's oldest licensed commercial pilot. He passed away in Winnipeg on April 8, 1966. Years later, others surpassed his record, but few logged as many adventurous flights in bush airplanes and airmail carriers.

Probably no one enjoyed his profession as much as the young Englishman who arrived in Canada to homestead but went on to fly his beloved north country. In his lifetime, Burton saw aviation grow from a shaky fledgling start through regular trans-Atlantic scheduled flights to the beginning of the space age. He acknowledged, with wonderment, that he was lucky enough to have experienced the most exciting era in history.

Appendix

Type and Registration of Aircraft Flown by Edward C. Burton

TYPE: Curtiss JN-4
Registration:
C-137; C-164; C-166; C-172; C-182; C-192; C-197; C-215;
C-232; C-233; C-241; C-243; C-245; C-247; C-249; C-251;
C-254; C-260; C-261; C-268; C-276; C-278; C-282; C-303;
C-306; C-309; C-310; C-318; C-322; C-324; C-327; C-329;
C-332; C-333; C-334; C-368; C-374; C-375; C-375; C-376;
C-378; C-410; C-419; C-420; C-421; C-422; C-423; C-424;
C-427; C-427; C-438; C-442; C-448; C-453; C-455; C-459;
C-476; C-557; C-567; C-712; C-713; C-715; C-719; C-720;
C-721; C-722; C-756; C-757; C-758; C-758; C-763; C-780;
C-781; C-782; C-783; C-784; C-785; C-786; C-788; C-802;
C-803; C-812; C-813; C-815; C-1010; C-1042; C-1324; C-
1328; C-1329; C-1341; C-1346; C-1347; C-1380

TYPE: Avro 504
Registration:
D-3356; D-6763

TYPE: Avro 594B Avian IVM (Avro 616)
Registration:
CF-CDT; CF-CDW

TYPE: Curtiss HS-2L
Registration:
G-CAOB; G-CAOC; G-CAOD

TYPE: Curtiss C-1 Robin
Registration:
CF-AHE

TYPE: De Havilland DH60G Gipsy Moth
Registration:
G-CALE; G-CAVK; G-CAVW

TYPE: De Havilland DH60X Moth
Registration:
G-CAJU; G-CAKC; G-CAKD; G-CAKE; G-CAKF;
G-CAKR; G-CAKS; G-CAKU;
G-CAPA; G-CATF; G-CAUB; G-CAUD; G-CAVF;
G-CAVH

TYPE: De Havilland DH-60M Moth
Registration:
CF-CAA; CF-ADP; CF-AGC

TYPE: De Havilland DH-80A Puss Moth
Registration:
CF-AGY

TYPE: De Havilland DH-83 Fox Moth
Registration:
CF-API; CF-ATV

TYPE: De Havilland DH82C Tiger Moth
Registration:
5907 RCAF

TYPE: De Havilland DHC-2 Beaver
Registration:
CF-OBU; CF-OBW; CF-OBX; CF-OBY; CF-OBZ;
CF-OCO; CF-ODA

TYPE: Canadian Vickers Vedette I
Registration:
G-CAND

TYPE: Fairchild FC-2
Registration:
G-CANB; G-CANC; G-CANF; G-CATA; G-CATR;
G-CATS

TYPE: Fairchild 71
Registration:
CF-AAK; CF-AAT; CF-AAX; CF-ACO; CF-ACY; CF-AET

TYPE: Fairchild 71C
Registration:
CF-AWU

TYPE: Fairchild FC-2W2
Registration:
G-CAIW; G-CART; CF-AHG; CF-AKT

TYPE: Fokker Super Universal
Registration:
G-CAWB; CF-AJF

TYPE: Pitcairn PA-6 Super Mailwing
Registration:
G-CAWF

TYPE: Travel Air SA-6000-A
Registration:
CF-AJO

TYPE: Travel Air BM-4000
Registration:
CF-AKV

TYPE: Buhl CA-5 Airsedan
Registration:
G-CATO

TYPE: Buhl CA-6 Standard Airsedan
Registration:
NC1771

TYPE: Stearman C3B
Registration:
G-CARR

TYPE: Stearman 4EM Junior Speedmail
Registration:
CF-AMB; CF-AMC

TYPE: Stearman 4EM
Registration:
CF-ASE; CF-ASF

TYPE: Eastman E-2 Sea Rover
Registration:
CF-AST; CF-ASW; CF-ASY

TYPE: Curtiss-Reid Rambler I
Registration:
CF-ABY

TYPE: Taylor E-2 Cub
Registration:
CF-ARA

TYPE: Waco YKC-S
Registration:
CF-AWH; CF-AWK

TYPE: Fleet 50K Freighter
Registration:
CF-BJU

TYPE: Stinson SR-9FM Reliant
Registration:
CF-BGM; CF-BGN; CF-OAV; CF-OAY

TYPE: Noorduyn Norseman
Registration:
CF-OBG; CF-OBI; CF-OBL; CF-OBO

A Short Description of Aircraft Flown by Ed Burton

Curtiss JN-4 (known as the Jenny)—the most frequently used World War II training airplane. A Canadian-built three-place version was the Canuck. Burton flew ninety-three JN-4s or variations during elementary training, as instructor or wreck retriever on various stations. A number were released to early commercial operators and barnstormers after the war. Power was the OX-5 engine, although individual owners experimented with other engines.

Avro 504 and variations—a somewhat rickety airplane that came along after the Jenny. The type never became popular in Canada, probably because other aircraft became readily available. Engines ranged from 80- to 120-hp. As a seaplane, these aircraft used a large central float and wingtip floats.

Avro 594 and 616—these were variations of the 504. Burton encountered them in Eastern Canada and Northern Quebec but never learned to love them. The early A. V. Roe aircraft were English designed and not always suitable for Canadian conditions.

Curtiss HS-2L—cumbersome flying boats designed by Glen Curtiss; first flown as military observers and later in Canada for forestry work. The Liberty engine provided 400- to 450-hp. Cooling water for the radiator was pumped up from the leaky hull. Instability in rough weather required a second pilot. In 1924, Burton crashed an H-boat in severe turbulence in which both passengers were killed and he was disabled for several years.

Curtiss C-1 Robin—a three-place high wing monoplane popular with private flyers but also used as a light duty bush airplane. Burton flew one for Bill Davis at Amos Airways in northern Quebec. Aircraft of the twenties and thirties were not commonly described by the number of seats of "places" they had. It was a matter of what could be squeezed in, and who was flying the machine. For example, both the Robin and the Fox Moth have been stated to be three- or five-place aircraft by different old-timers who flew them.

De Havilland DH60G Gipsy Moth; De Havilland DH60X Moth; De Havilland DH60M Moth—closely related single-engine, two-place biplanes, popular as trainers and observation aircraft. These airplanes were ubiquitous in the 1930s.

De Havilland DH80A Puss Moth—this three-place, high-wing monoplane was not strongly built and consequently never became a pilot's favorite.

De Havilland DH83 Fox Moth—two or three passengers could squeeze into a separate cabin between the wings and ahead of the pilot's legs. Burton flew one on the Pelee Island mail run from Leamington during winter 1943.

De Havilland DH82C Tiger Moth—manufactured by the hundreds and served as primary trainers during World War II. A few are still in use in 1998 as movie props, as they lend themselves well to being dressed up and disguised. Burton flew them as trainers in World War II during winter when forestry flying ceased.

De Havilland DHC-2 Beaver—a light transport accommodating pilot and six or seven passengers and designed in consultation with experienced bush pilots. It was a complete departure from anything de Havilland built previously, being a closed cabin, all-metal monoplane powered by a Pratt & Whitney 450-hp engine. Hundreds were built in Toronto and widely sold. It was one of Burton's favorite airplanes. The Ontario Provincial Air Service purchased many.

Vickers Vedette I—a biplane flying boat. Burton was flying a Vedette near Jackfish Island on Lake Nipigon when it shed two exhaust stacks back through the pusher propeller. On another occasion (also over Jackfish Island), a cylinder cracked in flight but Burton managed to land safely in protected water. He removed the offending cylinder and rod, capped the hole with a piece of plywood whittled from the floor, and taxied sixty miles to MacDiarmid at the south end of the lake. The last of the type, G-CAND, met its end in a windstorm while on the shore of the St. Mary's River in 1943. The Pratt & Whitney engine was put into a Sikosky flying boat where it lasted only eight hours before dying.

Fairchild FC-2; Fairchild FC-2W2 (and many variations)—a high wing tube and fabric monoplane with a 220-hp Wright Whirlwind engine. This high-utility machine could haul freight or pilot and four passengers, gaining favor in commercial service because of its versatility. Burton flew this type on airmail service and in northern Quebec.

Fairchild 71 and 71C—basically a bigger brother of the FC-2, although it came along later. The 420-hp Pratt & Whitney engine was more than adequate to haul a half-dozen passengers and gear. Burton flew this type on airmail service, on wheels and later for Bill Davis in northern Quebec on floats and skis. For part of one season, he flew a seaplane 71 for the Ontario Provincial Air Service. He thought this to be the best all-round bushplane of its time.

Fokker Super Universal—the Fokker was a Dutch design used extensively in general aviation in Canada. These rugged machines were ideal as freighters. A closed cabin and cabin heat were appreciated features.

Pitcairn PA-6 Super Mailwing—a biplane made specifically for airmail service; it was a Stearman look-alike.

Travel Air SA-6000-A; Travel Air BM-4000—early airmail biplanes, forerunners of the Stearman, powered by 200-hp Wright Whirlwind engines.

Buhl CA-5 Airsedan; Buhl CA-6 Standard Airsedan—five-place closed cockpit airmail machines occasionally flown by Burton. The Ontario Provincial Air Service in Sault Ste. Marie manufactured a variation in the 1930s. The Buhl was powered by a 300- or 400-hp engine and configured to carry a pilot and four or five persons. Even on a good day, Buhls would not climb higher than 2,000 feet on floats and consequently were not highly regarded.

Stearman C3B, 4EM Junior Speedmail, 4EM—designed by Boeing, these types were used by airmail services in Canada and the U.S. This aircraft was also a barnstormer, stunter and spray plane.

Eastman E-2 Flying Boat (also known as the Detroit Sea Rover)—sixteen were built. Powered by a 165-hp Challenger engine consisting of two three-cylinder radials bolted together; it was not one of Glen Curtiss' better efforts. Inadequate engine mounts eventually brought most to grief. Five flew from Detroit to the Yukon on a gold seeking expedition in 1932. Burton landed one on wet grass.

Curtiss Reid Rambler I—built in Cartierville, this sturdy Moth look-alike never really caught on, its competition being not other aircraft but the depression.

Taylor E-2 Cub—a low-powered high wing monoplane of forgiving disposition much favored by flying clubs in the 1930s, including the Windsor Flying Club where Burton instructed. Coauthor Ted Burton's first flight at the age of two was in a Taylor Cub from Windsor to Detroit.

Waco YKC-S—another popular biplane of the late 1930s powered by radial engines of 250-hp and up. Burton chose a Waco in preference to a cumbersome Fleet Freighter for the expedition to the Northwest Territories in 1939.

Fleet 50K Freighter—a twin-engined biplane designed as a freighter. Burton flew one and rejected it for the Northwest Territories expedition with Mosher and Burge, choosing instead the smaller, nimbler Waco. Only a few were built and most bit the dust in short order.

Stinson SR-9 Reliant—this airplane was part of the well-respected Stinson line. Usually engined with the 420-hp nine-cylinder Wright, it flew with engines as low as 285-hp. It was highly versatile and flown by movie stars and bush operators on wheels, skis and floats. Burton flew several with the Ontario Forestry Branch in the early 1940s at Red Lake and Fort Frances.

Noorduyn Norseman—a single-engined fabric-covered freighter beloved by all who flew it. The Norseman went through seven "marks," or models. First flown in 1935, approximately forty still function in Canada in 1998.

Bibliography

Books

The Birth of Western Canada: A History of the Riel Rebellions, by George F. G. Stanley (Toronto, Ont.: University of Toronto Press, 1961).

The Bremen, by F. W. Hotson (Toronto, Ont.: CANAV Books, 1989).

Canada's Flying Heritage, by Frank H. Ellis (Toronto, ON: University of Toronto Press, 1954).

Canadian Airmen and the First World War: The Official History of the Royal Canadian Air Force, Vol. 1, by S. F. Wise University of Toronto Press, Department of National Defence and Canadian Government Publishing Centre, 1980).

The Canadian Civil Air Register, by J. R. Ellis (Willowdale, Ont.: Canadian Aviation Historical Society, 1972–75).

The Doctor Rode Side-Saddle, by Ruth Matheson Buck (Toronto, Ont.: McClelland and Steward Limited, 1974).

Frank Barr, Bush Pilot in Alaska and the Yukon, by Dermot Cole.

History of Saskatchewan and The Old North West, by Norman Fergus Black (Regina: North West Historical Company, 1913).

125 Years of Canadian Aeronautics: A Chronology, 1840–1965, by G. A. Fuller, J. A. Griffin, and K. M. Molson (Willowdale, Ont.: Canadian Aviation Historical Society, 1983).

Pioneering in Canadian Air Transport, by K. M. Molson (Winnipeg, MB: J. M. Richardson & Sons, 1974).

The Royal North-West Mounted Police. A Corps History, by Captain Ernest J. Chambers (Montreal: Mortimer Press, 1906).

Saskatchewan A History, by John H. Archer (Saskatoon: Western Prairie Producer, 1980).

Unpublished Sources

Wheels, Skis & Floats, by Edward Cherry Burton, the unpublished manuscript of author's flying career.

Unpublished letters to Lucille Burton by Edward Cherry Burton, May, 1932, to August, 1932, courtesy of Mrs. E. C. Burton.

Journal of a Country Lawyer
Crime, Sin and Damn Good Fun
E. C. (Ted) Burton
5½ x 8½, 240 pp. SC
ISBN 0-88839-364-4

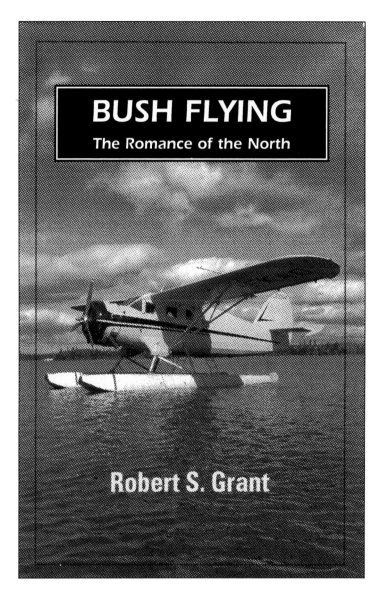

Bush Flying
The Romance of the North
Robert S. Grant
5½ x 8½, 288 pp. SC
ISBN 0-88839-350-4

Great Northern Bushplanes
Robert S. Grant
5½ x 8½, 224 pp. SC
ISBN 0-88839-400-4

MORE GREAT HANCOCK HOUSE TITLES

History

Cariboo Gold Rush Story
Donald Waite
ISBN 0-88839-202-8

The Craigmont Story
Murphy Shewchuck
ISBN 0-88839-980-4

Curse of Gold
Elizabeth Hawkins
ISBN 0-88839-281-8

Early History of Port Moody
Dorathea M. Norton
ISBN 0-88839-197-8

End of Custer
Dale T. Schoenberger
ISBN 0-88839-288-5

Exploring the Outdoors
Eberts & Grass
ISBN 0-88839-989-8

Guide to Gold Panning
Bill Barlee
ISBN 0-88839-986-3

Guide to Similkameen Treasure
Bill Barlee
ISBN 0-88839-990-1

Gold Creeks & Ghost Towns
Bill Barlee
ISBN 0-88839-988-X

Gold! Gold!
Joseph Petralia
ISBN 0-88839-118-8

Logging in B.C.
Ed Gould
ISBN 0-919654-44-4

Lost Mines and Historic Treasures
Bill Barlee
ISBN 0-88839-992-8

The Mackenzie Yesterday
Alfred Aquilina
ISBN 0-88839-083-1

Pacific Northwest History
Edward Nuffield
ISBN 0-88839-271-0

Pioneering Aviation of the West
Lloyd M. Bungey
ISBN 0-88839-271-0

Yukon Places & Names
R. Coutts
ISBN 0-88839-082-2

Northern Biographies

Alaska Calls
Virginia Neely
ISBN 0-88839-970-7

Bootlegger's Lady
Sager & Frye
ISBN 0-88839-976-6

Bush Flying
Robert Grant
ISBN 0-88839-350-4

Chilcotin Diary
Will D. Jenkins Sr.
ISBN 0-88839-409-8

Crazy Cooks and Gold Miners
Joyce Yardley
ISBN 0-88839-294-X

MORE GREAT HANCOCK HOUSE TITLES

Descent into Madness
Vernon Frolick
ISBN 0-88839-300-8

Fogswamp: Life with Swans
Turner & McVeigh
ISBN 0-88839-104-8

Gang Ranch: Real Story
Judy Alsager
ISBN 0-88839-275-3

Journal of Country Lawyer
Ted Burton
ISBN 0-88839-364-4

Lady Rancher
Gertrude Roger
ISBN 0-88839-099-8

Ralph Edwards
Ed Gould
ISBN 0-88839-100-5

Ruffles on my Longjohns
Isabel Edwards
ISBN 0-88839-102-1

Where Mountains Touch Heaven
Ena Kingsnorth Powell
ISBN 0-88839-365-2

Wings of the North
Dick Turner
ISBN 0-88839-060-2

Yukon Lady
Hugh McLean
ISBN 0-88839-186-2

Yukoners
Harry Gordon-Cooper
ISBN 0-88839-232-X

Outdoor Titles

12 Basic Skills of Flyfishing
Ted Peck & Ed Rychkun
ISBN 0-88839-392-X

Adventure with Eagles
David Hancock
ISBN 0-88839-217-6

Alpine Wildflowers
Ted Underhill
ISBN 0-88839-975-8

Birds of North America
David Hancock
ISBN 0-88839-220-6

Eastern Mushrooms
Barrie Kavasch
ISBN 0-88839-091-2

Guide to Collecting Wild Herbs
Julie Gomez
ISBN 0-88839-390-3

Northeastern Wild Edibles
Barrie Kavasch
ISBN 0-88839-090-4

Orchids of North America
Dr. William Petrie
ISBN 0-88839-089-0

Roadside Wildflowers NW
Ted Underhill
ISBN 0-88839-108-0

Sagebrush Wildflowers
Ted Underhill
ISBN 0-88839-171-4

Tidepool & Reef
Rick Harbo
ISBN 0-88839-039-4